ISBN 149235550X

EAN 9781492355502

"Let our advance worrying become advanced thinking and planning."

—Winston Churchill

CONTENTS

PREFACE

Robert C. Huber is the founder of USG, Inc., a company actively engaged in providing effective planning for emergency recovery.

Rex L. Pickett is a free-lance writer with extensive training for recovery from the effects of weapons of mass destruction.

In 1984, a major regional bank burned to the ground on Thanksgiving Day. Just days before the fire, a "plan" had been put into place by a small team for the first time. Previously, this type of plan had been called "contingency planning." The team from the bank called it a "disaster recovery plan," and it worked.

Over the next few years, the idea spread, and, although many companies had plans for smaller scale issues, and referred to those plans as "contingency plans," ideas and terminology began to change. Terms such as Disaster Recovery Plan, Crisis Management Plan, Business Contingency Plan, Business Continuance Plan, Business Resumption Plan, gradually settled on being named Business Continuity Plan, the standard of today.

Because of needless losses from companies not having a sufficient plan in place or workers trained, organizations to foster disaster recovery began to emerge in most states. An example of one such organization was called the Minnesota Security Interest Group (MSIG). The moderator of the new organization was the person who developed the successful recovery plan used to recover the regional bank that burned in 1984. He and members of the bank's recovery group spread the word around the country with slides and video to encourage other institutions to develop similar plans. MSIG changed its name a couple years later to the Minneapolis Contingency Planners Association (MCPA). It is now called the Business Continuity Planners Association (BCPA).

Business Continuity Planning (BCP) is the term to describe the process used to recover all of the essential business operations in a facility or campus.

BCP includes the essential operations of the associated Information Technology (IT) or Information Systems (IS) Department that the business relies on for performing its essential business operations.

Companies struck by some type of debilitating disaster that requires employees to relocate to alternate work locations must act immediately because every hour it takes them to reorganize and mobilize makes recovery more difficult. Regardless, recovery within a reasonable time frame is not possible without a plan.

To be able to recover within a specified time frame, the company needs to create a recovery plan, train its recovery teams to accomplish the recovery, and make it possible to identify disaster related and recovery related costs. When the plan has been completed and tested, a detailed document describing the plan can be made to meet audit requirements and ensure compliance with mandated regulations.

The success of a recovery plan depends on how well people on recovery teams are trained and whether or not they have conducted exercises and practiced their plans. Rehearsal under ideal conditions will demonstrate how long the recovery process takes. Then you add in the chaos factor, the fear factor, and the fact some of your trained recovery team members may not be able to function under difficult conditions or are absent. At that point, the recovery team will understand how difficult the recovery process is, how long recovery will actually take, and how important it is.

USG, Inc. is a company that provides business continuity planning, training, and certification. We primarily serve larger U. S. companies and government agencies. We believe it is our job as a company to keep up with the requirements and standards imposed on our clients to ensure they can actually recover after an incident, and do it in an acceptable time frame. We have created, developed, and use a standard methodology that helps clients comply with business requirements, regulations, and auditing.

The standard methodology decides what can and must be done for any given situation. To do so, it must meet some absolute requirements. It must be appropriate, reasonable, and possible within a pre-determined time frame. Certainty of success is ensured by always staying within the limits of span of control. Span of control is a form of defining the limits of a leader's effectiveness and designating an appropriate scope for the leader's unit. Span of control limits the number of persons on a team, the number of teams in a unit, the number of units in a section, the number of sections in a division, the number of divisions in an organization. The number is always no fewer than three, no more than seven. Span of control is the underlying philosophy of the standard methodology.

The standard methodology works because:

IT GETS THE NECESSARY DONE IN TIME!

CHAPTER 1

FRAMEWORK FOR RECOVERY

Introduction to Business Continuity Planning

The first five years of the twenty-first century witnessed two horrendous events, the attack on the Twin Towers and Hurricane Katrina. No two events more clearly outlined the dimensions of disaster. No two events caused so many unnecessary victims. No two events more clearly demonstrated the need for objective decision making, planning, and preparation. No two events so clearly showed the benefits of training as demonstrated by fire and police in New York, the U. S. Navy, and Coast Guard.

These two catastrophes were so different: one man-made, one nature's wrath; one confined to a small area, one spread over thousands of miles; one spanning 102 minutes, one spanning 102 hours; it would seem there is no commonality, but there is.

The first responders to both events performed feats of heroism bordering on the legendary. Firemen and police responded immediately in New York. The U. S. Coast Guard and U. S. Navy responded in the gulf coast area as soon as it became humanly possible. They did so because they were trained and cultured to do so. They saved thousands of lives. More lives could have been saved in New York if the police and fire departments could have communicated, but they didn't have adequate systems.

More people could have escaped had there been more stairways, but changed building codes reduced the number of stairways required.

Thousands of people in New Orleans had no means to evacuate. Others trusted the levees and didn't go away. When the levees failed, as some predicted they would, it was too late to make use of a train and the busses that could have carried thousands of people to safety. Ignoring the warnings, because they had ridden out hurricanes before, turned out to be very dangerous for those who stayed because the storm was as powerful as predicted.

Both events have generated hours and hours of investigations and hearings to assign blame, but assigning blame prevents nothing, nor reduces the effects of future events, however such disastrous events might come to pass.

There are some obvious lessons learned from both events. Response must be immediate. Responders must know what they are doing, and must be able to communicate with one another. Response must come from somewhere else. Those lessons help us decide where we go from here. Anyone who chooses to do so may prepare for difficult times. State and local governments and many companies are required by federal and state law to do so.

Managing the aftermath of a disaster or crisis is extremely difficult and will have unpredictable results unless serious planning is done prior to the event and a simple but solid plan is activated immediately after the event.

The differences between man-made and natural events are worth noting. Man-made events tend to be smaller, of shorter duration, with effects more clearly defined, and possibly might be preventable. Natural events affect much greater areas with effects more varied and numerous, are slower to develop and last longer, are predictable, but not preventable. The common element is that there is a means of coping with whatever might occur.

Clear recognition of what type events can happen, preparation for the possible effects, careful selection of organized response, and training of people to respond sensibly to adversity can significantly reduce, even prevent, the effects of disaster. The important activities are planning and training.

The first issue for business continuity is one of compliance with the many laws, regulations, and standards in effect today. Most companies must be able to recover their core operations within seventy-two hours or they will not comply with requirements and rulings of government agencies and current laws. Lack of compliance can be very disruptive and expensive. All companies should ask their legal departments and auditors to prepare an opinion to define the company's compliance requirements. Appendixes A and B list many of the existing public laws and regulations that mandate disaster recovery plans.

In some cases, because of the legal principle of vicarious liability, IT operations managers are subject to criminal prosecution and penalties as well. Officers of corporations and IT managers have been prosecuted for providing false information, or for knowingly not complying with government regulations, when those laws and regulations made it mandatory to maintain and supply current, accurate information.

Capability of recovery depends almost entirely on planning—recovery personnel, equipment, recovery site, communication, and, most importantly, recovery team training. Training! Training! Training! Communication with clients, regulatory agencies, employees, etc. is also critical. When you can articulate to auditors who, what, when, where, and how you are prepared to recover after a disaster, and they accept your plans, you've done it all. With any one of those elements missing, you may be non-compliant and/or unable to recover and may have to face consequences.

Preparing to deal with the aftermath of a disaster requires several steps.

1. Identify a location for carrying out critical business operations
2. Identify a place for IT/IS to re-establish essential computer operations
3. Prepare for recovering backed-up or lost data
4. Prepare for reconnecting users to that data
5. Train recovery teams so they can act immediately upon notification
6. Obtain all necessary permissions to carry out recovery operations prior to disaster
7. Plan how cash transactions will be made under disaster conditions
8. Notify clients, employees, regulators, investors of the situation
9. Manage the actual crisis
    - Protect the good name of the victim company
    - Respond to media, regulators, investors, employees
    - Counsel those who were there when disaster hit
    - Counsel those who must recover IT/IS under stressful conditions
    - Counsel those who must recover all other critical business operations
    - Manage contractual obligations under emergency conditions

The success of a recovery plan depends on how well those teams—IT and Non-IT—are trained, and whether or not they have practiced recovery activities (conducted exercises) so they understand how long it actually takes for the activity they must provide. Add in the chaos factor, the fear factor, and the fact that some of your trained recovery team members may not be able to function under those conditions–or they may be victims themselves, which may negatively impact the recovery operations. If the emergency recovery activation call arrives at 3:00 a.m. and one or more of the recovery team members being relied upon to recover essential services has children, this may cause a delay if this contingency is not built into the plan.

As insurance company losses for business interruption have risen and regulations requiring recovery plans have increased, new expectations dictate standardized plans covering all critical departments within a company, organization, or agency. Auditors, insurers, regulators, and investors now expect individuals involved in the recovery process to be trained and team exercises conducted.

Although the requirements for comprehensive plans have increased, the difficulty to produce them has not. If you cannot explain the following in a very small paragraph, recovery will be more difficult:

- How your company will recover critical operations
- How your company will keep clients, media, employees, and investors informed
- Who the individuals are who will roll up their sleeves and provide the actual recovery work

Just plan a step-by-step recovery process, document it, keep it simple so everyone understands it, and you're nearly there.

Take the time to create a short list of things you need to do during the recovery—call them responsibilities, then attach a team name to each responsibility.

Next:

1) Add in what you need to get the job done
2) Where you will do it
3) Identify gaps
4) Determine how to fill in the gaps
5) Add more people to the equation—such as contracted employees

Concerning recovery time: If all of the critical operations of your organization can be restored within seventy-two hours or fewer, your plan will satisfy most time requirements automatically.

Concerning cost, look at it this way: Calculate what your company would lose in revenue, penalties, contract default, and litigation, versus the cost to recover, and you have your budget requirements nicely laid out in front of you.

One of the more important costs in your budget will be for training. Training provided by outside organizations varies from organization to organization and region to region.

Some organizations are very good at providing training at a basic level. Their classes include teaching standard terminology and providing general concepts, which are accepted by most, that have been created by other organizations over the years. Other organizations provide more in-depth training along with their certification process and usually offer CEU credits, as well as an industry certification. Such in-depth training usually includes:

- Extensive training in the interviewing process to gather the correct—not the most—information necessary to recover a business unit
- How to create and conduct training exercises for recovery team members, which is now an HIPAA requirement
- When, why, and how to update the recovery plan and the recovery plan document (The document itself is primarily a manual when used to train, and is used as a guidebook during an actual recovery.)
- How the teams should be formed based on the type of business structure
- Special training to determine the actual dollar loss per hour during the recovery period, as well as cost to recover, etc.

A company that provides this level of training should be staffed with instructors holding degrees in computer science or who have MBAs or Ph.D.s in relevant disciplines. Verify the credentials of the company you choose for training, especially the instructors. Determine if they hold certificates, degrees, etc., or are consultants that have retired from some other job, and are doing this as a side job. Most training costs are about the same, so it's worth choosing the best available. Remember: Ask for references.

If you would like to determine which training is right for you, check the recommendations of some of the major insurance companies that insure client companies for business interruption insurance. Large insurance companies often select a recommended provider for business continuity planning and training. They provide that contractor's name to their underwriters and agents to recommend a consultant for clients who are seeking business insurance. Insurance companies are particular in their recommendations because it is the insurer who is at risk if their insured cannot recover in a reasonable amount of time.

If you choose a company to help you develop a plan or train your recovery teams, choose one that will provide references with names and phone numbers and show you actual samples of their work. If the company is trusted by a client, the client will permit use of their document as a sample.

For many years, planning for recovery from disaster was concentrated around IS/IT systems. As disaster recovery matured into business continuity planning, emphasis has changed to recovering the entire business operation using a standard approach. The importance of this detailed planning is illustrated in the words of Dwight D. Eisenhower, thirty-fourth President of the United States: **"Planning is priceless."**

Planning for Emergency Recovery

This book is about preparing a structured plan to enable emergency recovery in an organized and orderly manner. The plan will have provisions for:

1. Accounting for everyone
2. Activating the recovery plan
3 Mobilizing recovery teams
4. Notifying the recovery site(s) of activation
5. Notifying off-site storage providers of impending activity
6. Completing emergency recovery tasks in an orderly fashion
7. Maintaining the health and safety of the recovery team
8. Releasing appropriate information about the disaster
9. Monitoring regulatory requirements
10. Preparing for a return to normal

Response! Planning and Training for Emergency Recovery, provides the necessary education and leadership skills to successfully create and implement a business continuity plan. Through group interaction and practical application of these processes, an individual should have the confidence and competency to develop a fully comprehensive recovery plan. With diligent application, business continuity will become an integral part of the corporate or government agency culture.

Why Business Continuity Planning Is Important

Business Continuity Planning (BCP) is important because of the financial and psychological impact on organizations, communities, and people without it. Our purpose is to provide information that will help you avoid those consequences. If you are experienced, you may see an easier or another way to do what you are already doing. Business continuity planning has made great strides in recent years. For people who are new to BCP, we're going to give you information and guidelines on how to start building your disaster recovery plan. But to get into that, we need some definitions.

Disaster: An event that disrupts an organization's ability to perform critical business activities.

Business Recovery: Actions taken to restore essential business functions.

Recovery Plan: A sequence of actions decided in advance to restore essential business functions in an acceptable length of time.

Do not confuse a disaster recovery plan with a disaster recovery plan document; they are two different things. A plan is a series of intended activities. A document is only a printed description of the plan.

A rather interesting statement came from someone at the University of California at Berkley in 2001: "More data will be created in the next three years than throughout all previous human history." This incredible amount of information we are creating increases daily. Fortunately, we have places to put it. We have disk drives that are so big we can actually put all that data someplace. But so what? The so what is that this information is what we live by; these are things that make our cars run, our phones ring, get us our paychecks—all the things we have to do to live. And that data needs to be connected to people, not just computer hardware. That's the key. No matter what you think about disaster planning, business continuity planning, and disaster recovery planning for IT, it's getting that information connected to people that's the most important thing.

> The primary objective of a business continuity plan is to identify what needs to be accomplished immediately after a disaster strikes.

So what's the chance that a disaster will ever occur to you?

Life in our times, wherever in the world we live, work, or play, contains a number of possible happenings we call risks.

Risks

- Natural Disasters
- Human Error
- Crime
- Civil Unrest
- Terrorism
- Noncompliance

From among those risks the possibilities for disaster are very likely. The most common are weather related.

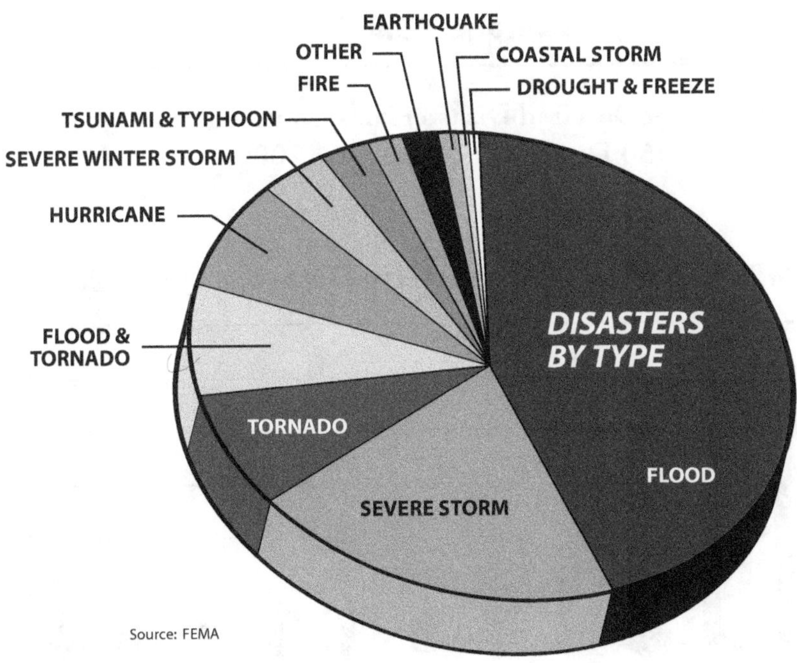

In recent years the United States reorganized its efforts for mitigating disasters. Criteria for designating an event as a disaster were brought up to date. The Federal Emergency Management Agency (FEMA) has the ability to maintain and publish statistics that show a much more defined picture of the frequency of disastrous events.

Major FEMA Disaster Declarations & Major Fires

Year	*Declarations*
1990	38
1991	43
1992	45
1993	32
1994	36
1995	32
1996	75
1997	44
1998	65
1999	50
2000	45
Average: 45.9	

FEMA's Number of Declared Disasters has Continually Increased To 154 Disasters For The Year 2005.

Natural Disaster Occurrence by Disaster Type (2004)

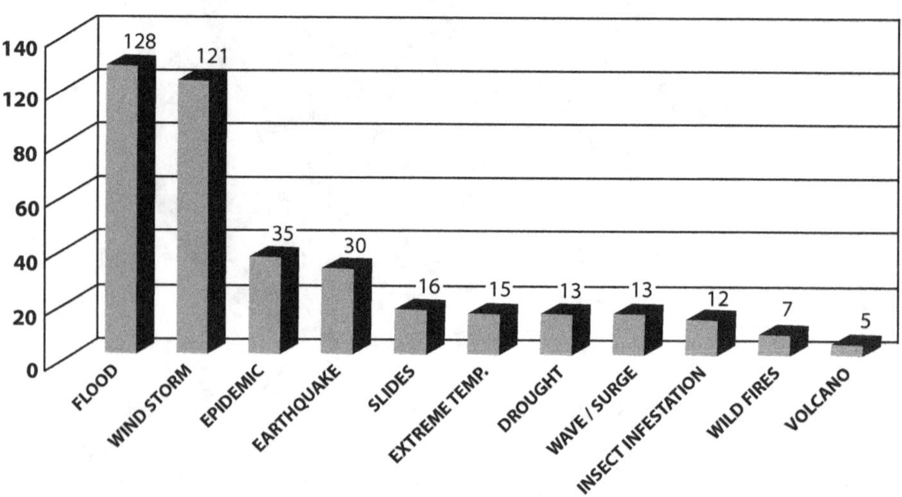

Source: "EM-DAT: the OFDA/CRED International Disaster Database—www.em-dat.net—Université Catholique de Louvain—Brussels—Belgium"

The scope and distribution of costly damage is demonstrated by this chart of Billion-Dollar Weather Disasters.

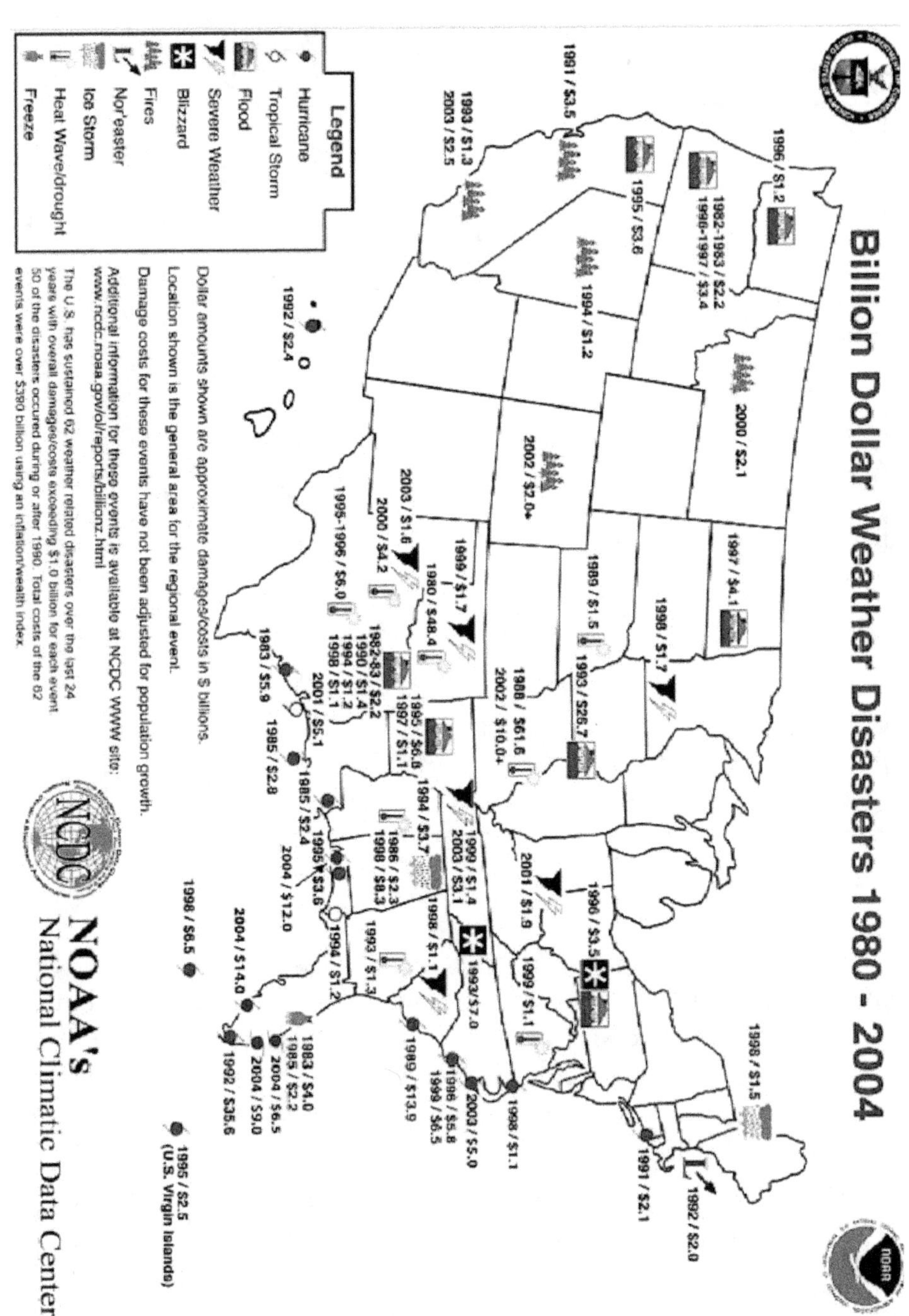

This chart shows how Pennsylvania was affected by the severe rain storms and flooding during the spring of 2005:

FEMA-1587-DR, Pennsylvania
Disaster Declaration as of 04/14/2005

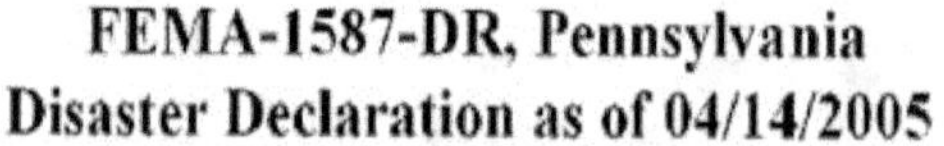

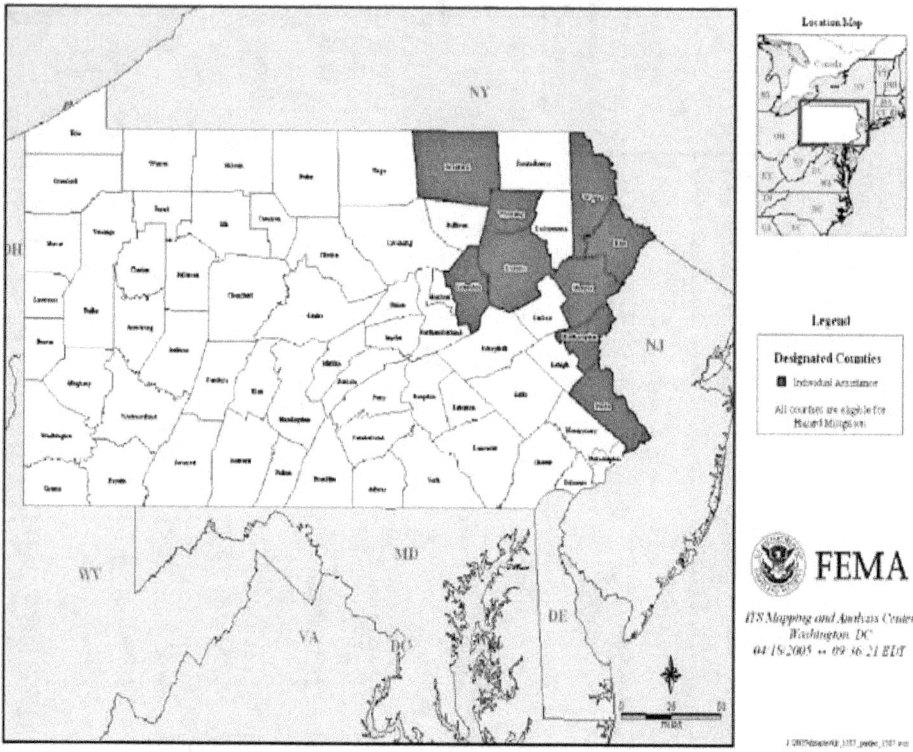

Adverse weather not only shuts down businesses, it may prevent your key employees from getting to operating or recovery sites. You have to build that into your disaster recovery plan. Your plan should provide for an alternate person taking care of those critical tasks that must be done by someone. Cross training may be the answer. Having good documentation of your plan both on and offsite is also important.

There are many risks other than weather that we face daily. They have varying degrees of probability. Simple human error can result in extensive damage because of domino effect in breakdowns. The potential for damage and destruction is very real from criminal acts that are often accompanied by vandalism. Civil unrest can cause disruption of transportation and public utilities and may require evacuation from a particular area. Terrorism will usually cause limited damage and disruption, but can create an aura of fear and uncertainty that can be just as damaging and extensive as a bad storm. Noncompliance with laws and regulations can result in unexpected shutdowns and very expensive penalties.

Countless businesses have closed, eliminated employees, or have irreparably damaged their reputation because of an event that rendered their operation useless for a period of time for which they were not prepared. Recovery of critical operations within a predictable period is essential for a vast number of reasons ranging from compliance and contractual agreements to lost revenue and client confidence.

So what's your risk? Does it really matter? Yes, it does. You have to plan for recovery whatever the disaster might be, but clear understanding of the risks enables planning to reduce threats and their effects. Risk assessment will also help tailor your plan to the more evident probabilities.

Compliance: For those of you who are new in the disaster recovery/business continuity discipline, there are requirements for business recovery planning that are mandated by public laws, rules of regulatory agencies, and best practices by various business associations. Appendixes A and B list the common ones and the general activities they require. All companies should get opinions from their legal departments and auditors to be certain their company is in compliance. Operational contingency plans are required in most regulated industries. Liability often depends on whether the implementation plan is reasonable. Reasonable today means standard. You might have the ability to plan things that are new and exciting, but make sure you have all the standard procedures included. *Do not ignore the obvious.*

Closely related to compliance is litigation. Litigation is very damaging and expensive. It's the activity that often causes the greatest money loss; you can lose your building, you can lose your income from your business for a length of time; contracts can get you in trouble if you can't perform as those contracts require. In the litigation world, you can get past most litigation issues if you can show a developed plan, the plan is standard, and you have conducted training exercises.

There is a common denominator in all of these risks. Whatever the cause—hurricane, flood, fire, crime, civil unrest—the end result is downtime. Not only is downtime expensive, it is a double-edged sword. The company loses revenue, and there are costs to recover. As you consider the ramifications of the following chart, consider also the impact on the workforce, which might be as irreplaceable as the property damaged or washed away.

Disaster Always Causes Revenue Loss

The following chart shows that Fortune 1000 companies are very vulnerable to business interruption. Companies experiencing delays in recovering core business operations can expect to lose massive amounts of revenue if recovery or critical business operations extend over many days or weeks.

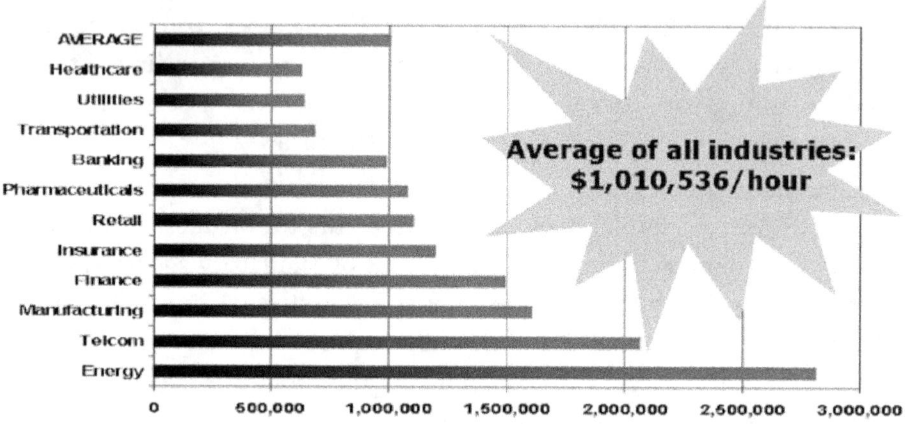

Regardless of the average, downtime for Fortune 1000 companies is hugely expensive for any large company. That's why companies are saying "Now is probably a good time to start creating a plan to recover."

The next question: If downtime is so expensive, how about recovery costs? When we go out to a client, we start forming teams and looking at IT capabilities and uses because IT has become so critical to everyone and everything. Some of the very first questions we ask are "What do your servers look like? How many do you have that are actually critical to production and revenue generation? If they all go down, how long will it take you to bring them all back up? The main frame? How long? Are there any dependencies? Can you walk down a row of thirty servers, click the on switch and start them all up at the same time?" To date, we haven't found a client able to do that. They all say, "No, we have to start this server first, then load the data from that one to these ones..." and so on. Technical people know this.

Our experience has shown us this: If a company tells us they have one thousand servers, it usually comes out that three hundred are critical. If they have ten, three are critical. So there is a cost of recovery just to restore your servers—both in money and time. Even though IT people are doing a marvelous job of getting service restored, the organization's operational departments may not be able to use the systems until everything is up and running. So this is another real cost that raises a significant question. Do you have data or special software you're going to need right away? If so, maybe it should be on a disk, maybe it should be stored. That's an example of a decision that has to be made.

There are several types of intangible losses that don't show up right away: task flow, reduced market share, confidence loss, loss in investor confidence, employee uncertainty. These all relate to cost of recovery. There have been a number of surveys published on this topic. The University of Minnesota conducts such surveys each year. These surveys have shown a network outage extending over forty-eight hours could put 20 percent of Fortune 500 companies out of business within two years if a plan to begin recovery was not executed immediately.

Another survey says, "The average time to recover from a disaster is three to five days." So if you have a disaster, and you are not prepared, it's telling you pretty clearly that you are probably not going to recover very well. For the expectation of recovery after a disaster without a disaster plan, only 43 percent of those companies will ever resume operations, and, of those, only 25 percent will be in business two years later. You get around these eventualities by planning for them.

So how do you go about planning to cope with disaster?

This process narrows it down to eight steps:

- **Step 1**: Identify the business continuity coordinator (BCC)—who's going to be the boss of the recovery effort. Identify the business issues—list the critical business functions and prioritize them.
- **Step 2**: Identify each business unit's recovery responsibilities and tasks. Identify the recovery time requirements, prioritize those requirements, and determine the business unit dependencies. Priority of the necessary is important.
- **Step 3**: Identify subject matter experts who will help you create this recovery strategy and plan. Determine the business unit requirements for offsite storage, and identify the work group recovery environments.

- **Step 4**: Collect appropriate recovery documentation for IT operations. Determine applications needed and priorities. List data forms required. Document the system software.
- **Step 5**: Identify all inter-dependencies between business units. Select team leaders, identify recovery locations, assign recovery locations by work group because some groups will have special needs. Sometimes all units can be together. Consider the cost; do what makes sense for your organization. Estimate the downtime costs by function, business unit, and time.
- **Step 6**: Identify application restoration requirements. Document the restore procedures by plan form. You may have to synchronize the data with certain applications. Document recovery scripts. Add them in an appendix.
- **Step 7**: Calculate the time it takes to restore the hardware. Calculate the time to restore and synchronize the data. Identify outside storage procedures, identify inventory, create a business phone list, gather together maintenance contract information. Include all customer numbers. Have them in your document.
- **Step 8**: Finalize the document. Identify procedures for document control. Number the documents and account for all the numbers. When it's time to update these, perhaps every three months, call a meeting. Bring in all your team members and leaders and have them turn in the old document. Issue them the new one and have them sign for it. Use only printed copies so you know who has which version. Schedule recovery exercises and actually do them. Evaluate them later as things change in your company.

Disaster Definitions

Business Continuity (BC) The process of returning essential services to an acceptable level of operation after a disaster.

Business Continuity Document The printed and published copy of the business continuity plan. It is used as a manual for training recovery team members and as a guidebook during an actual disaster.

Business Continuity Plan A set of arrangements and procedures decided in advance that enable an organization to respond to a disaster and resume its critical operations within a defined time frame.

Clustering A process that defines critical functions and operations quickly to enable establishment of a business continuity organizational structure to facilitate recovery.

Contingency Organization The collection of persons selected as business continuity coordinator (BCC), BC team leaders, and BC team members for business continuity activities.

Disaster An event that disrupts an organization's ability to perform critical business functions.

Risk Possible events that can cause disruption or destruction such as: natural disasters, human error, crimes, civil unrest, terrorism, or non-compliance.

Note: See Appendix C for additional definitions

Disaster Declaration

A disaster declaration is made when an interruption results in a decision to mobilize a portion of or the entire emergency recovery contingency organization, and to initiate a recovery of some or all of the interrupted operations functions at a recovery site.

Initial disaster notification can come from:

- Building security
- Police or fire departments
- Computer operations personnel
- Other employees
- Customers/clients

A business continuity plan should include documented and tested procedures that, if followed, will assist in ensuring the availability of critical resources and in maintaining the continuity of essential operations during an emergency situation. It should aid in organizational stability through an orderly recovery process in the event of significant problems and interruptions. A business continuity plan is not intended to be a procedure manual to perform all functions. It should include *only those high priority tasks required* to efficiently recover essential operations immediately after a disaster.

The plan should be designed to handle a worst-case interruption, i.e., total destruction of the company facility or campus. In reality, however, problems occur in varying degrees. Each situation requires careful consideration before a decision can be made regarding disaster qualification. The contingency organization should be structured so that competent and knowledgeable management personnel are placed in the evaluation role. The business continuity coordinator is expected to qualify the disaster and activate or select the level of the disaster to be declared. In order to make a realistic decision, the disaster duration should be a realistic estimate and not an optimistic expectation. Certain factors and criteria affect the qualification process, and they must be weighed to decide whether to mobilize all or only part of the contingency organization. Some considerations may include the following:

- Time period, day of the week or month, time of the year
- Accounting requirements, peak processing period, etc.
- Nature of interrupting event and confidence in estimated time to repair
- Nature of threat, e.g., bomb scare or actual event
- Non-data-center-related event, i.e., caused by widespread communications failure, earthquake, toxic gas exposure, etc.

Reliance is placed upon the business continuity coordinator to ascertain the degree of disaster and to offer the most reliable estimate for its resolution through the activation of all or only part of the contingency organization.

Once the business continuity coordinator determines the best estimate of recovery time, the business continuity coordinator should immediately mobilize the contingency organization and invoke the recommended level of disaster.

Disaster Levels

Disaster levels are used to quantify the length of an interruption and the time frame in which a disaster declaration decision must be made. Each plan should be designed around the critical time frames established for the recovery of critical operations.

Each disaster level requires a separate set of actions. All plans should provide for communicating the severity of the interruption to automatically form the basis for the type of recovery actions appropriate to the interruption.

The ultimate objective is to rapidly define the disaster. Defining the disaster establishes the criteria for declaring the disaster level and swiftly activating the appropriate response team or teams.

Selecting a Disaster Level

The selection of a disaster level is based on the time estimated to correct the interrupting event. By establishing a generalized disaster plan of multiple time levels, it is possible to select an appropriate recovery response without having to state pre-defined actions for every potential cause of interruption.

The time levels are pre-defined and used in disaster level determination as depicted in the following table:

Level	Who can declare	Description
Level One—Problem (up to 24 hours)	Operations Manager or Shift Supervisor	Minor equipment breakdown, partial loss of network, major program error, contaminated databases. There is no modification to the scheduled workload of the unaffected systems. Little or no mobilization of the contingency organization is needed.
Level Two—Emergency (24–48 hours)	Business Continuity Coordinator or Executive Management	Moderate damage to facility and/or the computer equipment is observed, but normal operations can be resumed within 24 to 48 hours. Partial mobilization of the contingency organization may be needed.
Level Three—Disaster (over 48 hours)	Business Continuity Coordinator or Executive Management	Major facility and/or computer equipment damage is observed, with interruption in operations for over 48 hours. All functions and personnel are moved to a recovery site(s). Full mobilization of the contingency organization is indicated and a disaster is declared.

Disaster Assessment

When a disrupting event occurs, the following sections contain steps that should be followed for some common problems, although these lists do not necessarily represent the order in which they are to be implemented. For emergencies, all areas of reporting and notification should be addressed. A complete listing of emergency response personnel and contact numbers should be included in the call-up chart.

Computer Hardware Failure

If any apparent malfunction of computer hardware could significantly impact operations, the following steps should be considered:

- Verify the computing equipment is down or malfunctioning
- Notify the appropriate manager
- Secure assistance as necessary
- Determine if operations can continue without the malfunctioning unit
- Direct the operations staff to continue operations, if possible, with the malfunctioning unit offline
- Notify the equipment maintenance personnel (vendors, personnel, etc.) of the problem
- Notify the BCC if operations cannot continue

Software Failure

If any apparent malfunction of the operating system, applications, and data could significantly impact operations, the following steps should be considered:

- Verify the failure of the software
- Notify the appropriate manager
- Ensure support personnel solve the problem as quickly as possible
- Advise systems personnel of the problem
- Restore system software and resume normal operations when the failure has been repaired
- Notify the BCC if operations cannot continue

Equipment Failure

If any apparent malfunction of equipment (e.g., power) could significantly impact operations, the following steps should be considered:

- Verify the existence of equipment failure
- Notify the appropriate manager
- Secure the assistance of appropriate maintenance personnel to alleviate the problem
- Provide estimated downtime
- Notify the BCC if operations cannot continue

Communication Equipment Failure

If any apparent malfunction of communications equipment could significantly impact operations, the following steps should be considered:

- Verify the existence of communication equipment failure
- Notify the appropriate manager
- Secure the assistance of the technical services team as required
- Direct the staff to continue operation, if possible, with the communication equipment disabled
- Provide downtime estimates
- Notify the BCC if operations cannot continue

Summary of Emergency Procedures

Upon notification that a disaster has occurred and that the group is operating under temporary emergency conditions, the following disaster level tables outline the order of events.

The disaster levels are defined by the following criteria:

Disaster Level—One

Step	Responsibility	Description
1.	Employee	Notifies the supervisor immediately of problem.
2.	Supervisor	Confirms the problem, determines appropriate action, and estimates length of time to resolve.
3.	Supervisor	Notifies managers that normal operations may resume.

Disaster Level—Two

Step	Responsibility	Description
1.	Employee	Notifies the supervisor immediately of problem.
2.	Supervisor	Identifies that a level two disaster has occurred and immediately notifies the business continuity coordinator.
3.	Business Continuity Coordinator	Confirms level of disaster, determines appropriate level of action. Contacts the recovery management team members, thus activating the business continuity plan. If necessary, the business continuity coordinator provides the time and place to set up a command center and provides additional instructions regarding other employees and the use of the recovery site.
4.	Team Leaders	Call all team members and provide instructions on address, meeting location, and any other information from the business continuity coordinator, upon notification that the business continuity plan has been activated. It is not necessary for any employee to confirm the disaster or level of disaster after initial notification.
5.	Team Members	Report their findings and estimates only to their team leaders, who are their points of contact. This prevents multiple versions of loss estimates or inconsistent recovery information from reaching the business continuity coordinator.
6.	Business Continuity Coordinator	Determines that operations can safely and productively return to the main facility or some other permanent location. Until determination is made, operations continue under the temporary emergency conditions.
7.	Business Continuity Coordinator	Notifies managers that normal operations may resume and all teams may be disbanded.

Disaster Level—Three

Step	Responsibility	Description
1.	Employee	Notifies the supervisor immediately of problem.
2.	Supervisor	Identifies that a level three disaster has occurred and immediately notifies the business continuity coordinator.
3.	Business Continuity Coordinator	Confirms level of disaster; determines appropriate level of action. Contacts the disaster management team members, thus activating the business continuity plan. If necessary, the business continuity coordinator provides the time and place to set up a command center and provides additional instructions regarding other employees and the use of the recovery site.
4.	Team Leaders	Call all team members and provide instructions on address, meeting location, and any other information from the business continuity coordinator, upon notification that the business continuity plan has been activated. It is not necessary for any employee to confirm the disaster or level of disaster after initial notification.
5.	Team Leaders	Provide clear instructions to their team members. These instructions include: • Obtaining damage estimates • Estimating salvage probabilities • Performing salvage operations • Estimating recovery time • Setting up operations at the recovery site • Resuming operations under emergency conditions
6.	Team Members	Report their findings and estimates only to their team leaders, who are their points of contact. This prevents multiple versions of loss estimates or inconsistent recovery information from reaching the business continuity coordinator.
7.	Team Leaders	Update the business continuity coordinator at regular intervals.

Step	Responsibility	Description
8.	Business Continuity Coordinator	After the initial operations are under way and preliminary salvage assessments have been made, some teams may be disbanded. However, the contingency organization is still in effect until operations are stabilized at all recovery locations.
9.	Business Continuity Coordinator	Determines that operations can safely and productively return to the main facility or some other permanent location. Until determination is made, operations continue under the temporary emergency conditions.
10.	Business Continuity Coordinator	Notifies managers that normal operations may resume and all teams may be disbanded.

Announcing a Disaster

If external announcements require responses to the media, a public information spokesperson, who is part of the crisis management team, shall inform the media appropriately. The public information spokesperson has responsibility for all media communications. Media communications are typically approved by the legal department prior to responding to the media.

The business continuity coordinator, with input from recovery team leaders and with the approval of executive management, prepares any preliminary announcement. Announcement considerations may include:

- Initial assessment of problem
- Extent of damage, if available
- Possible causes, if available
- Who reports to work
- Where and when to report to work
- Where employees should direct questions
- Information about employees' personal belongings at work
- When detailed disaster information will be available

Business Continuity Planning and Training Process

The following represents the process flow of the Business Continuity Plan (BCP).

Key Elements of Business Continuity Planning

1. Identify essential personnel
2. Identify critical business functions
3. Conduct a clustering exercise to establish critical business operations
4. Track revenue flow through business units
5. Create recovery teams
6. Identify key recovery team responsibilities
7. Identify key recovery team tasks
8. Develop recovery team training exercise
9. Conduct team training exercise
10. Produce recovery document

As the Recovery Process Conceptual Flowchart shows, it is essential to properly plan the recovery process prior to implementing a plan that follows best practices. **Commitment** from senior management is a must and continued sponsorship throughout the organization is only possible if management supports the importance of planning for the continuity of operations. Considering the fact that BCP is a fiduciary responsibility of all public companies and organizations, getting initial support may be the easiest task.

Establishing initial management support is only the first step. Developing continued support by ingraining business continuity into the culture of the company or organization takes the total commitment of senior management, and once obtained, it will be easier to establish the process flow.

Recovery

The Recovery Process: A Conceptual Flowchart

This plan uses a team approach. It is structured so each team has a specific function. The Recovery Process Conceptual Flowchart identifies the sequence of events expected to occur during the recovery process. The careful identification of logical recovery events are the elements that will bring about, not just a recovery process, but a very efficient, orderly, and, above all, swift recovery.

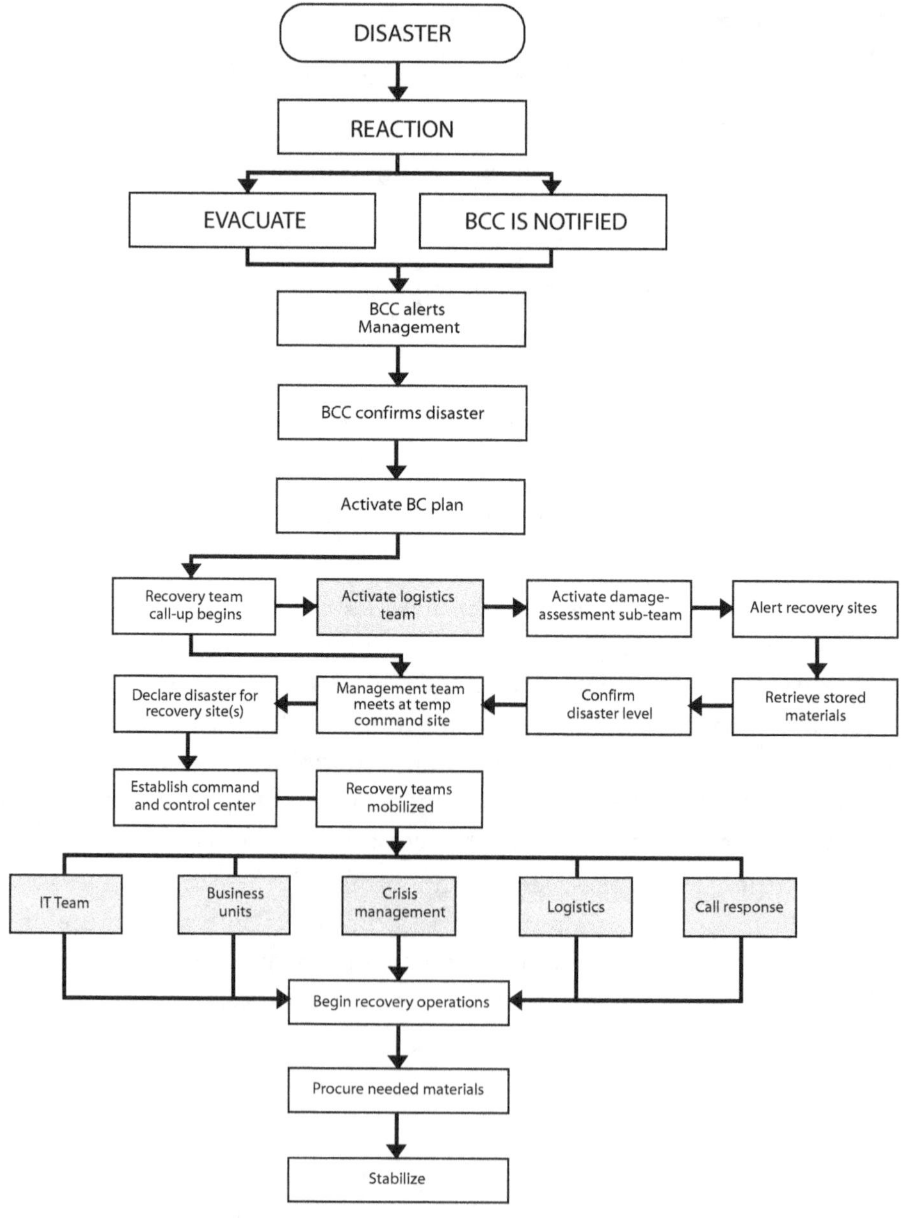

Sample Development Phases

Phase One

- Identify recovery coordinator
- Identify departments
- List critical department functions
- Prioritize functions
- Identify team leaders

Phase Two

- Identify department recovery responsibilities and tasks
- Identify recovery time requirements
- Prioritize department requirements
- Identify department dependencies
- Select team members

Phase Three

- Identify subject matter experts
- Determine department requirements for off-site storage
- Identify workgroup recovery requirements

Phase Four

- Identify application software
- List software by priority/platform
- Identify data files/databases
- List data by priority/platform
- Identify critical/essential data
- List by priority, platform, workgroup
- Document system software
- List servers by priority, location, and dependencies

Phase Five

- Identify recovery location(s)
- Determine recovery location by workgroup and department
- Estimate downtime costs by function, departmental unit, and elapsed time

Phase Six

- Document restore procedures for each department
- Identify essential services restoration requirements
- Identify specific documents required to carry out business at their location
- Identify IT downtime tolerance
- Calculate time to restore and sync data

Phase Seven

- Identify off-site storage procedures
- Identify off-site storage inventory
- Obtain vendor list and phone numbers
- Gather vendor maintenance contract information
- Obtain employee phone list

Phase Eight

- Finalize plan document
- Identify document maintenance and control
- Schedule recovery exercises
- Conduct training exercise
- Evaluate training exercise

Identifying Company Recovery Capability

Executive managers have a fiduciary responsibility to review their operations to ensure their ability to respond to adversity. Before a time of crisis, we suggest that executives at all companies ask the following questions of their management team. The answers will aid them in determining how rapidly they can respond to calamity and how long it will take them to restore normal operations.

Who to Ask	Question or Area of Review
Executive Management Team	Are procedures in place for contacting each other and making critical decisions? Do you have a command center for the management team to discuss activities and communicate? Do all executives understand their altered roles to be performed at time of disaster? Who would be their successor in the event they are unavailable?
	Review insurance policies to ensure adequate coverage.
CIO	What is the state of recovery plans? Are they comprehensive and current?
	Do we have backups completed regularly for critical data on major systems or workstations within the business units?
	Revisit physical protection, user authentication, access control, encryption, security management for networking, and communications.
	Discuss possible contracts for replacement equipment or quick-ship of assets from technology vendors.
	Do we have our mission-critical applications replicated at an alternate location? Can we update information quickly on our web site in the event of a disaster?
Communication Manager	Review the public relations and corporate communications procedures.
Risk Manager	Revisit physical protection, user authentication, access control, encryption, security management for networking, and communications.
	Review security management or access procedures to buildings.
	Are procedures in place for mailroom deliveries, identification of outside vendors, who to contact, what type of identification is required?
	Review insurance policies to ensure adequate coverage.
	How will we access facilities after disaster? Do we have arrangements or pre-planning with the fire and police departments?

Who to Ask	Question or Area of Review
Purchasing	Discuss possible contracts for replacement equipment or quick-ship of assets from technology vendors.
Customer Support	How would our customers contact us in the event of an outage? Have we redirected call traffic to an alternate number?
Customer Support Manager	Who are our key customers and suppliers? Where is contact information for them? Is it stored off-site?
Travel	What alternatives are there for travel—mail, paging, video-conferencing?
Department Managers	What critical paper documents do we have? Do we have copies imaged electronically or hardcopy duplicates stored off-site?
	What are the procedures to remove building and systems access to former employees or consultants? How often are access lists reviewed and cleaned out? Do we have procedures for evacuating the disabled? Are procedures used to grant access to facilities and systems appropriate and complied with? Do employees know who to contact to report suspicious activities? Do employees know what to do to respond to an emergency? Do employees have family crisis plans, including local meeting places and out-of-state relatives as points-of-contact? Do company contingency plans include employee family concerns such as temporary childcare?
Records Management Manager	How are critical non-electronic documents protected and where are they stored? Are copies of critical documents taken and stored off-site?

Who to Ask	Question or Area of Review
Facilities Manager	Review security management or access procedures to buildings.
	How will we access facilities after disaster? You may want to have a discussion or pre-planning meeting with fire and police departments.
	Review procedures for mailroom deliveries, identification of outside vendors, who to contact, what type of identification is required.

Sample Timeline

The following timeline is a sample of a typical project plan for a corporation. It is very important to establish major milestones prior to an engagement. All major milestones are pre-planned, recognized, and discussed prior to the engagement kickoff meeting.

ID	Task Name
1	Project Kickoff
2	Identify Recovery Site
3	Develop Recovery Process Methodology
4	Identify Business Critical Operations
5	Prioritize Critical Business Operations
6	Identify Business Unit Subject Matter Experts
7	Identify IT Restoration Team Leaders
8	Conduct First Disaster Scenario Walk-Thru Exercise
9	Identify Business Critical IT Functions
10	Prioritize IT Functions For Recovery Sequence
11	Identify Transmissions Requirements
12	Choose IT Restoration Team Members
13	Identify Application Software and Recovery Tasks
14	Identify Hardware Recovery Tasks
15	Identify and Assign Communication Restoration Tasks
16	Identify System Startup Scripts and Jobs
17	Identify System Software Recovery Tasks
18	Determine Backup and Restore Requirements
19	Determine Off-Site Storage Requirements
20	Identify Recovery Teams Responsibilities & Create Task Lists
21	Determine Recovery Time Estimates
22	Identify Required Recovery Documentation
23	Identify Business Interface Requirements
24	Identify Logistics Requirements
25	Obtain Vendor Contact and Contract Information
26	Determine Data Management and Support Requirements
27	Identify Network Restoration Requirements
28	Develop Recovery Training
29	Create Plan Document
30	Distribute Plan
31	Structured Conference Room Walk-thru Exercise

The following diagram effectively summarizes the BCP process. The first seventy-two hours are critical to the future of the company or organization. After the first seventy-two hours, business processes can continue under emergency conditions utilizing an alternative facility. On average, it will take eleven weeks to return to normal business operations.

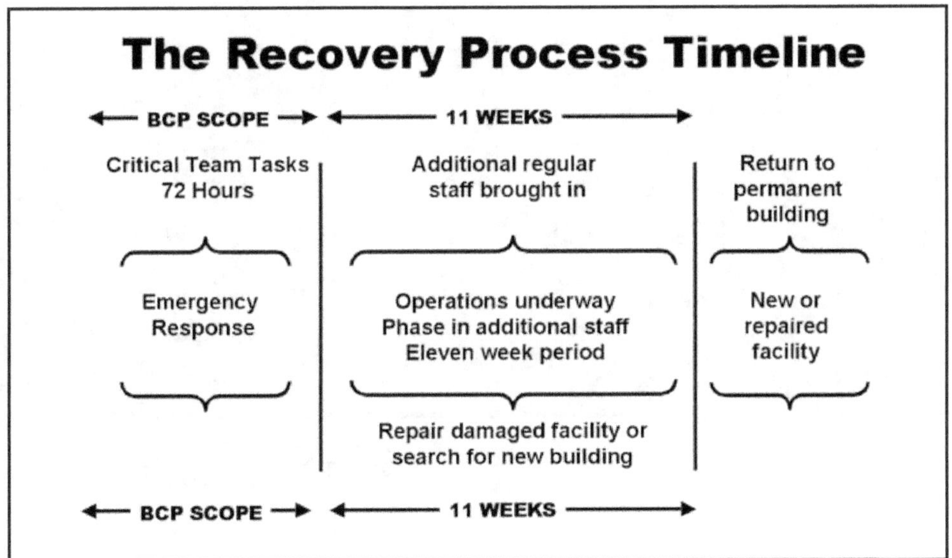

This first chapter, Framework for Recovery, defines business continuity, describes why it is important, establishes definitions, explains how levels of disaster are determined, outlines the process for planning and training, and shows how to determine recovery capability. It ends with a clear idea of how long the process of recovery could take. The remaining chapters all deal with specific concepts important to the overall process of business continuity. They are a series of building blocks. The order of their presentation is to encourage a sequence of completion that ensures successful recovery.

CHAPTER 2

RISK ASSESSMENT

Introduction To Risk Assessment

What Is It?

Risk assessment is identifying the possible events that might have an adverse effect on company facilities, operations, or personnel.

Why Is It Important?

Risk assessment is important to reduce the element of surprise, prevent stoppages of work and process, and prevent or limit damages.

Who Does It?

Risk assessment should be a constant effort for all employees. It requires all employees to be aware of what is going on around them for their own and the company's well-being.

Risk assessment for maintenance and operating purposes is the responsibility of executive management. It is generally the information base underlying company maintenance and security functions.

A formal risk assessment study would be compiled by the risk management department. Risk managers would be assisted by plant maintenance, engineering, operations, information systems, personnel, security, and legal departments. Such a study is the basic research about the organization and its properties to form a threat review.

Risk managers should receive any reports that relate to safety or security. Executive management should be able to request an up-to-date threat review report whenever one might be needed. Threat review reports should include weather reports of severe weather or any other information relative to events of potentially disastrous proportions.

Scope of Risk Assessment Activities

For business continuity purposes, risk assessment must consider those factors that affect your company's ability to conduct its normal business functions. It should consider the probable hazards that could result in disasters to company facilities or functions.

There are two extensive questionnaires included in appendix D—a sample physical security audit and a sample information security audit. They cover nearly any eventuality that must be considered. Answering the questions in the sample audits will provide a clear picture of your company structure. The information you will develop is important for use in these functions:

1. Compliance with regulations and standards
2. Business impact analysis
3. Identifying recovery capability
4. Business unit clustering
5. Recovery team development
6. Forming a recovery plan

Because each company is different, with varying operations and corporate cultures, the formula used to assign values to the individual questions of each questionnaire is left to the person conducting the assessment. The values decided should be tailored to support disaster recovery planning and activities.

Risk assessment must also consider factors outside of the organization's properties. Activities such as civil unrest, crime, terrorism, natural phenomena, and weather can pose substantial risk to an organization's properties, people, and operations.

A review of the history of local disastrous events will provide the information to form a list of possible threats and the probability of their recurrence. Local news and weather reports should be included as sources of threat information.

Threat Review Description

Included here is a form for making use of risk assessment information to maintain a current threat review. The form lists common disastrous events. It provides space for estimating the impact of potential events using the same criteria for designating disaster levels, the estimated time for recovery.

The **P** column is for assigning a probability factor: 1—Low, not likely; 2—Moderately likely, not often; 3—Very likely, often; 4—Certain, imminent.

The process starts with determining which events are possible and assigning an estimate of recovery time from the effects expected. The second step is assigning the probability of the event happening and how soon. From this, a picture will emerge that describes the threats your organization faces. From this review, management can make the decisions necessary to the well-being of the organization.

A threat review completed on an on-going basis could provide a disaster danger rating very similar to the fire danger rating published by many states that have significant forests and grasslands. The constantly changing weather environment, level of civility, and increasing levels of criminal and terrorist activity make maintaining a constant threat review advisable.

Threat Review

As of ______________________

		Level One		Level Two		Level Three	
	INTERNAL	P	24 Hours or Less	P	24–48 Hours	P	More than 48 Hours
POSSIBLE THREAT	1. Mechanical Failure						
	2. Power Failure						
	3. Labor Strife						
	4. Criminal Action						
	5. Fire						
	6. Security Breach						
		Level One		Level Two		Level Three	
	LOCAL	P	24 Hours or Less	P	24–48 Hours	P	More than 48 Hours
POSSIBLE THREAT	1. Weather						
	2. Floods						
	3. Chemical Spill						
	4. Riots						
	5. Terror Attack						
	6. Fire						
		Level One		Level Two		Level Three	
	REGIONAL	P	24 Hours or Less	P	24–48 Hours	P	More than 48 Hours
POSSIBLE THREAT	1. Weather						
	2. Floods						
	3. Weather Aftermath						
	4. Terror Attack						
	5. Large Area Fire						

Probability:

1—Low, not likely
2—Moderately likely, not often
3—Very likely, often
4—Certain, imminent

CHAPTER 3

BUSINESS IMPACT ANALYSIS

Introduction to Business Impact Analysis (BIA)

Business impact analysis (BIA) is a process that provides companies with a comprehensive financial analysis of business operations that helps identify potential exposures. Performing a BIA is often an integral part of business continuity planning. However, it is not necessarily a critical component of an actual planning initiative. This analysis does help identify the key business processes for a business continuity plan (BCP) by quantifying their continuity risk impact. Most often, a plan is created based solely on a worst case scenario.

Why Is It Important?

A BIA provides impact cost estimates which help when assigning priorities to emergency response efforts. Information grouped by location, for example, can define the scope required. It demonstrates that business needs are driving the recovery effort. It also aids understanding the loss over time that a disaster would cause which becomes valuable when seeking business interruption insurance.

A BIA tries to meet the following objectives:

- Identify key business processes by individual business units

- Provide information to expand key business processes with associated cross-training
- Quantify risks and exposures to help assign priorities to recovery efforts
- Evaluate high risks to reduce exposures, define insurance coverage needs, and ultimately reduce insurance premiums.

With data accumulated from each department or business unit, one can summarize the overall loss over time from each area. Analysis can identify the most critical areas to be included in the business continuity plan.

The most important result of a BIA process will be a clear recovery time objective (RTO) and a recovery point objective (RPO) that management can utilize to determine how much funding will be necessary to recover from a disaster under emergency conditions.

The process for a business impact analysis is laid out in a format that includes these parts:

Part 1—Overview of the Business Unit

Part 2—Work Flow Interdependencies

Part 3—LAN or PC Computer Resources

Part 4—In-house Computer Based Information Systems

Part 5—Outsourced Data Processing

Part 6—Regulatory and Legal Issues

Part 7—Transaction Volume Loss–Normal Business Day

Part 8—Transaction Volume Loss–Peak Business Day

Part 9—Revenue Loss

Part 10—Additional Expenses

Part 11—Embarrassment or Confidence Loss

Part 12—Client Loss

Sample Business Unit's External Dependencies

Sample Business Unit's Vital Records Needs

Sample Business Unit's Vital Electronic Records Needs

The forms to assist in completing a business impact analysis can be found in appendix E.

Business Impact Analysis Findings

All the information acquired and analyzed from risk assessment and business impact analyses can be sorted to form the data to be used for the clustering process. Significant exposures and critical functions will stand out. That information is used to make the findings for this form.

Significant Financial Exposures (List in recovery priority order.)

1. ____________________

2. ____________________

3. ____________________

4. ____________________

5. ____________________

Recovery Point Objective (RPO)

A recovery point objective (RPO) is the point where a process can be restarted with full intent to be kept running in an acceptable mode at an acceptable pace. Different processes, different devices, and different industries require very different start-up procedures. The varying conditions that define a recovery point objective cannot be designated until the interruption has occurred.

Recovery Time Objective (RTO)

The recovery time objective (RTO) is the period of time from a business interruption to the recovery of a service or process. The standard recovery time is seventy-two hours time or less. When an interruption has occurred, speed of response to restore becomes a critical factor in itself. Downtime is deterioration time. The longer a business function is unable to function, the longer it takes to restart and get back up to speed. The time objective will be to restart critical functions as soon as possible to stop any resources drain.

Recovery Strategy

A recovery strategy is the selection of necessary actions and the sequence in which to take them. Risk assessment and business impact analysis provide the information necessary to valid and timely decisions.

Recovery Strategy

1. ____
2. ____
3. ____
4. ____
5. ____

A clearly defined recovery strategy is the necessary guidance for compiling the information critical to an orderly recovery plan. A well thought out, orderly plan means a well thought out, orderly recovery. The recovery strategy is also guiding information to the clustering and interviewing processes described in following chapters.

CHAPTER 4

BUSINESS UNIT CLUSTERING

Introduction to Business Unit Clustering

Business Unit Clustering™ is a process designed to identify critical business units that must be recovered first in the event of a disaster. These critical business units represent the engine of the business continuity plan and ensure recovery of the company or organization. This type of recovery structure will include all essential business unit operations that must be recovered within the first seventy-two hours of a disaster.

This technique often makes use of risk assessment procedures and a business impact analysis (BIA) to help define and designate the most critical business functions. Defining and designating critical business functions is the foundation to a successful recovery plan.

The clustering process becomes the beginning element to a sound continuity plan.

Who Does It?

The clustering exercise is generally completed by a business continuity advisor collecting information from a group of subject matter experts who know the organization's structure well enough to discuss each individual area.

When Does It Need To Be Done?

The clustering exercise is the first step in developing a business continuity plan. Typically, the clustering exercise will establish the basis of the recovery structure. This information will be utilized in all further activities, including identification of recovery team leaders and team members.

How Does The Process Work?

The business continuity advisor asks each subject matter expert to list all departments within the company or organization. After all departments are listed, the business continuity advisor asks the subject matter experts to explain each department's role and its responsibility within the company structure. It is quite important that participants define process rather than protect territories. At this point, functions similar in nature, regardless of department, are clustered into a main business unit with similar responsibilities. Commonality of function is clustered to eliminate duplication and redundancy in favor of time. Speed of response is vital to prompt restoration of function.

If a department is determined to be vital to operations during the disaster recovery process, that department becomes one of the business units to be represented in the recovery structure as a team. If it is not considered critical to the recovery process, that department's activities will be designated for resumption later than the first seventy-two hours after a disaster.

What Is The Process Order?

The order in which the clustering process tasks are performed should be arranged to fit the management culture of the company. This will enable the contingency organization to take advantage of as many standard operating procedures (SOPs) as possible because people are more likely to do that which they have been trained to do. Within that mind-set, the order of the clustering functions will look something like this:

1. Determine recovery strategy
2. Designate business continuity coordinator (BCC)
3. Identify critical business functions
4. Cluster appropriate functions
5. Structure the recovery organization
6. Identify subject matter experts
7. Determine business unit priorities
8. Confirm disaster level parameters

9. Establish timetable of functional recovery
10. Finalize the contingency organization structure

Throughout this text and in the appendixes are a number of forms to aid the collection of information necessary to the clustering process. The information developed in risk assessment activities and business impact analyses can also be valuable in the clustering process. Understanding the interviewing, training, and team development processes greatly contributes to the success of assembling an effective recovery organization.

Basic Team Structure

An organization chart for the basic recovery team structure would look much like the **Call-up Worksheet**. It is displayed here to show the relationship of the basic recovery teams to executive management and the disaster management team. The legend **Call–up Worksheet** denotes that this is the starting point of developing the communication order for the response system.

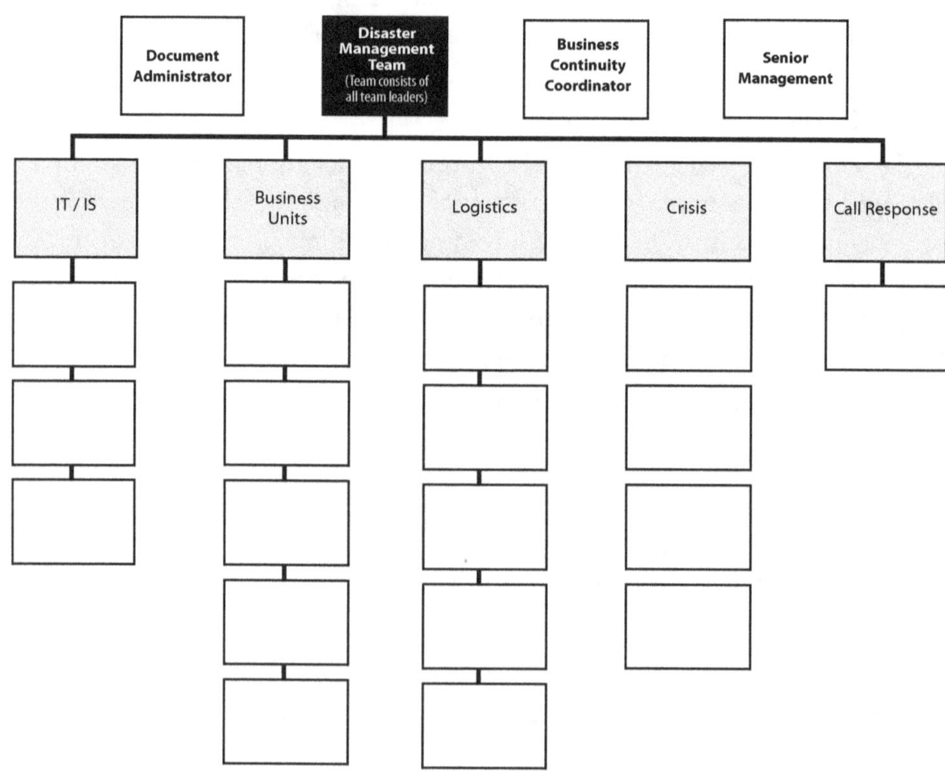

Sample Basic Team Structure

The following teams are those required to constitute an approved business continuity plan. Each team is expected to carry out specific functions. The order in which they are listed here is of no particular importance as these functions will usually be operating simultaneously.

IT Team

Sets up PCs on desks of business unit workers

Hardware	Software
Data	PC support
Communications	LAN
WAN	Phone

Business Unit Teams

Sales
Finance
Marketing
Supply Chain
Various product work groups

Crisis Management Team

HR/Payroll	Safety/Security
Legal	Media release

Logistics Team

Damage assessment and salvage

Purchasing	Vendor contact
Mail	Supplies
Shipping/Receiving	

Call Response Team

Answers incoming calls
Delivering approved messages

Team Activities

When the recovery strategy is formed, functions critical to recovery are defined and are then assigned to recovery teams.

Team Name: ______________________________

Team Leader: ______________________________

Responsibilities

#1 ______________________________

#2 ______________________________

#3 ______________________________

First Seventy-two Hours—Tasks A

#1 ______________________________

#2 ______________________________

#3 ______________________________

After Seventy-two Hours—Tasks B

#1 ______________________________

#2 ______________________________

#3 ______________________________

The information collected on this form is the initial step of the interviewing process. Each responsibility should break down into one or more tasks that must be completed in the seventy-two hour time frame. The next chapter, chapter 5 Team Interviewing, describes in detail how to conduct interviews and continue the process to gather the information necessary to effective recovery team development.

CHAPTER 5

TEAM INTERVIEWING

What Does The Interview Process Do?

The purpose of interviewing team members is to identify what specifically must be included in the recovery plan. This also defines the specific functions, responsibilities, and tasks of each individual area. USG, Inc., for example, uses a Socratic technique to develop information about each area's functional group.[1]

Why Is It Important?

By gathering specific information from each area, you can determine which functions are critical and how each fits into the business continuity plan. It also identifies dependencies with other groups or departments. When you complete these individual meetings, each team leader will understand their responsibilities to the plan and have identified specific tasks necessary to recover.

1. The Socratic Method used consists of a series of questions, the object of which is to elicit a sequence of answers that expresses the logical soundness of a concept or intended action.

Who Does It and When Does It Need To Be Done?

The process of interviewing each team leader and team member is the responsibility of the business continuity advisor or business continuity coordinator. The process of interviewing should run throughout the business continuity project. Usually the business continuity coordinator will establish a series of meetings to help coordinate a timely interviewing process.

Meetings should be run in a deliberate manner to ensure validity of the information gathered. Subject matter for meetings should generally follow the phases described in chapter six.

Sample Questions

Tell me about your area.

What are the functional responsibilities of your department?

How long a period of time can the company function without your department's services?

Where do you get your information?

How is the information transferred to you?

How time sensitive or critical is the information?

What information do you get from other areas or departments?

How important is your data to your employees?

How important is your data to your clients?

How long could your clients be without the data kept on your system?

Do you know how many business critical servers you have?

If your systems are down, what is the manual approach you would need to capture the information?

Interviewing Worksheet

This worksheet is designed to identify tasks and responsibilities. The information collected will be used to form the team templates. The questioner must assume a worst case scenario, a level three interruption. The most important aspect is making certain no functions are duplicated unnecessarily but all required tasks are completed.

After information has been collected, teams will meet separately to assign mandatory tasks to specific team members. Recovery teams should be able to describe their recovery strategies in a single page team plan. Sub-teams should make every effort to limit each team member's assigned tasks to a single page plan that expresses what must be done in simple terms. This is a significant factor in accomplishing recovery in seventy-two hours time or less. It also identifies information needed to specify training needs that are described in chapter seven.

Interviewing Worksheet

Date: ______________________________

Business Unit Name: ______________________________

Contact Name: ______________________________

Data Confidence Level: ______________________________

List customers and suppliers: Include a very short description of what they receive or what they supply. Rank them in order of importance.

Business Unit Customers
1.
2.
3.
4.
5.
Business Unit Supplier
1.
2.
3.
4.
5.

Business Interfaces

Explain the internal/external business interfaces performed by your department. Include categories such as type of external companies, agencies, vendors, banks, customers, and internal departments. Prioritize the interfaces according to disaster level.

Internal	Priority
1.	
2.	
3.	
External	**Priority**
1.	
2.	
3.	

Function Significance

Which tasks within this business process cannot be delayed or postponed during recovery processing? Note which business tasks and responsibilities are less critical to the recovery of your department. How long can they be delayed? Describe why they can be delayed, and the potential processing impact of each delay to your area, and impact to other areas (if known).

Function	Priority
1.	
2.	
3.	
Task	**Priority**
1.	
2.	
3.	

Comments:

____

____

____

____

Software/hardware Applications

Name the software/hardware applications that are required to support the business operations of your department. Include the name of the application and whether or not online access is required. Prioritize the applications according to disaster level. Compile a separate list for servers that includes a priority order for restart.

Process	Application	Priority	Online Access (Y/N)

Primary and Secondary Systems

Name the systems and provide a brief description of their function.

1. ____________________________________
2. ____________________________________
3. ____________________________________
4. ____________________________________
5. ____________________________________

Which tasks within this business process can be delayed or postponed during recovery processing? What business tasks and responsibilities are less critical to the recovery of your department? Can they be delayed? Describe why they can be delayed, and the potential processing impact of each delay to your area, and impact to other areas (if known).

Systems	Priority
1.	
2.	
3.	
Task	**Priority**
1.	
2.	
3.	

Comments:

Special Needs

List the special needs required by the critical business operations of your area.

Vital Records Storage and Retrieval

Name the record categories, storage location, retrieval procedures, and information about back-ups and alternates

1. ______________________________

2. ______________________________

3. ______________________________

4. ______________________________

5. ______________________________

Business Continuity Procedures (Action Plan)

List the current BCP procedures for this unit and date established.

1. ______________________________

2. ______________________________

3. ______________________________

4. ______________________________

5. ______________________________

Duration of Plan

List the period of time each procedure is expected to cover.

1. ______________________________

2. ______________________________

3. ______________________________

4. ______________________________

5. ______________________________

List current Standard Operating Procedures (SOPs).

Normal Procedures	Responsible Person Name, Title, Contact Information
Normal Procedures	**Responsible Person Name, Title, Contact Information**

Key Contacts and Resources—Internal Implementation—Disaster Management Team

1. ____
2. ____
3. ____
4. ____
5. ____

Responsible Persons—Possible Team Leaders

1. ____
2. ____
3. ____
4. ____
5. ____

Activators of Plan—Order of Succession

1. __________________________________
2. __________________________________
3. __________________________________
4. __________________________________
5. __________________________________

Return to Normal Operations

1. __________________________________
2. __________________________________
3. __________________________________
4. __________________________________
5. __________________________________

Resource Requirements

1. __________________________________
2. __________________________________
3. __________________________________
4. __________________________________
5. __________________________________

CHAPTER 6

RECOVERY TEAM DEVELOPMENT

What Is It and Why Is It Important?

Selection of the right teams is critical to the success of the business continuity plan. When the continuity team structure is established, selection of team leaders and team members comes next. If team leaders are assigned first, they can assist in identifying and designating team members. These individuals will form the company's organizational structure for the first seventy-two hours after a disaster and will have the primary responsibility to assure the survival of the company in the event of a disaster.

The selection of the right teams requires assigning the most knowledgeable subject matter expert to a specific team. That individual must understand the importance of the process and possess a positive attitude to ensure the business continuity process is properly executed. Generally, the executive leadership and team leader positions are represented by director or manager level positions within the organization.

Senior management will focus on the long-term recovery of a company or organization. Their responsibilities tend to be more strategic in focus, while the recovery team will concentrate on day-to-day functions and the immediate needs of the company.

Who Does It And When Does It Need To Be Done?

The initial selection of team leaders and members is made by the senior management of an organization. The selection of these individuals should be made immediately after the initial meeting with the business continuity coordinator and the business continuity advisor.

How Does The Team Development Process Work?

Recovery team development starts at the executive management level of the organization. The first line of an organization chart would look something like this:

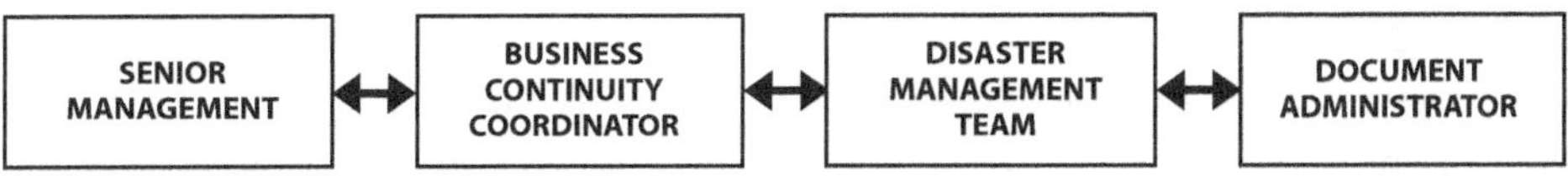

This group must perform the fundamentals of creating a business continuity plan (BCP). Logic suggests that creating and developing such a plan must be done in phases. The first phase is establishing the recovery strategy, communications, and infrastructure necessary to recovery activities. This phase includes selecting a suitable recovery site and appointing team leaders.

The next phase is assembling and developing the contingency organization. The clustering process identifies the groupings that will restore company operations. They will probably not reflect the regular company organization, but they will identify the functions absolutely necessary to recover from a severe interruption.

Business Continuity Teams

There are five primary functions that will become teams as the contingency organization is developed. Recovery plans defining these five functions will meet the compliance requirements for most industries. After being designated as a team they become the basic structure for recovery programs to be established. The following pages represent a sample of what the teams' makeup is within the five primary functions. This format is so universal that it should be the beginning format of all business continuity plans. This makes the contingency organization chart look like this:

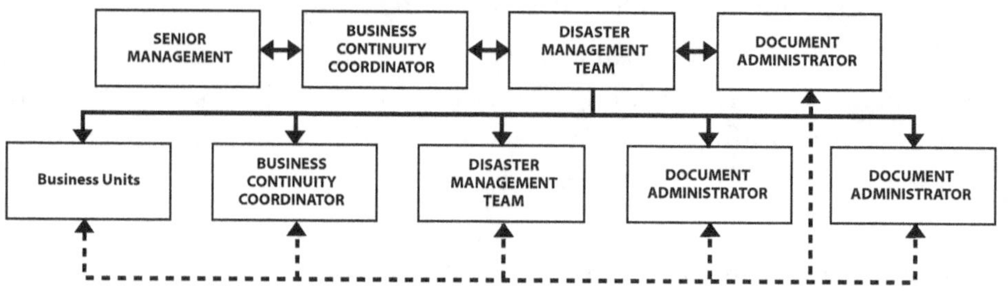

This basic structure creates an instant demand for leaders that meet special criteria, being subject matter experts in their respective fields. It also demands a phased approach so each of the teams can develop their structure and name their personnel independent of each other, and generally at the same time. From designation of functions, the next phase is identifying responsibilities within the functions. Responsibilities generate tasks, which can be assigned to specific individuals for completion. From this process a basic contingency organization is formed. At this point the several groups and sub-groups are designated as teams. The next chart is the basic contingency organization. This chart also forms the basis for initial notification of team members whenever a disrupting event happens.

Basic Contingency Organization

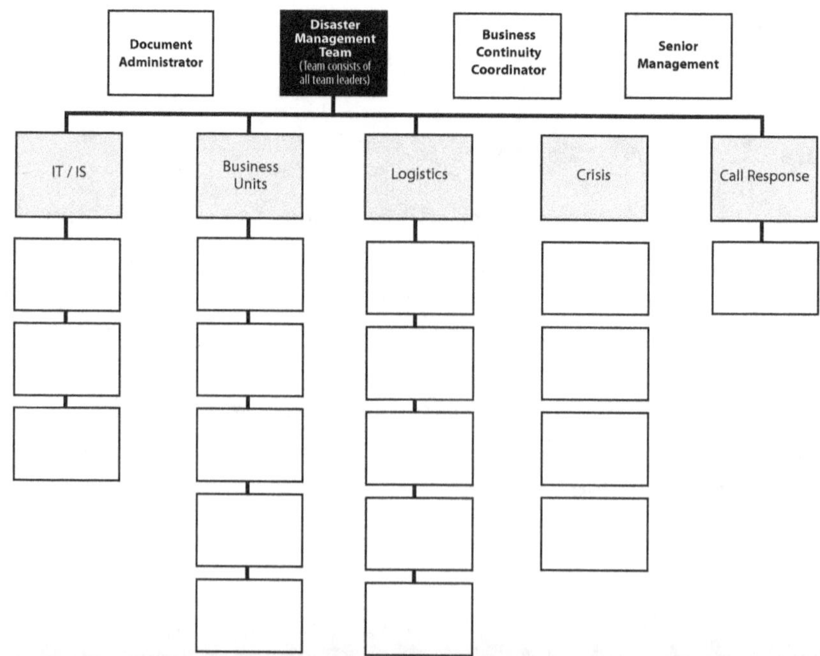

Each of the charts on the following pages shows several sub-teams clustered around the basic team. Each sub-team is a function discovered in the clustering process. Subject matter experts are identified in the clustering process also. The diagrams are intended to reflect how closely the sub-teams must work together to make certain their respective functions are accomplished as quickly, and surely, as possible. The sub-teams noted would each have a designated leader. The sub-team leaders make up the membership of the basic function team they are assigned to. The sub-teams noted in these charts are samples. Each organization that develops a business continuity plan would identify their respective functions, teams, and sub-teams.

Criteria for Subject Matter Experts to be Sub-Team Leaders:

1. Technical competence with emphasis in fundamentals
2. Passion for their expertise
3. Commitment to the organization
4. Awareness of coordination with other functions
5. A positive or "can do" attitude

Crisis Management Team Chart

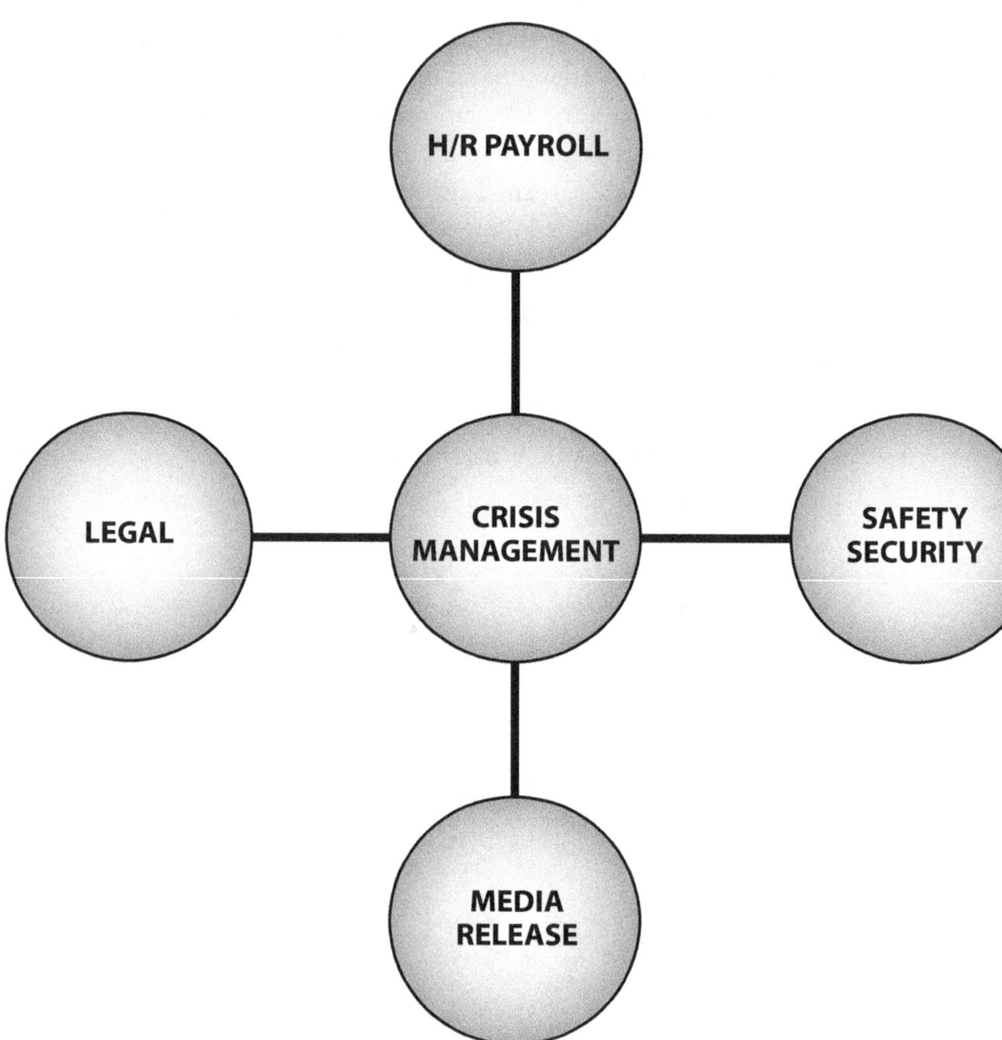

IS/IT Team Chart

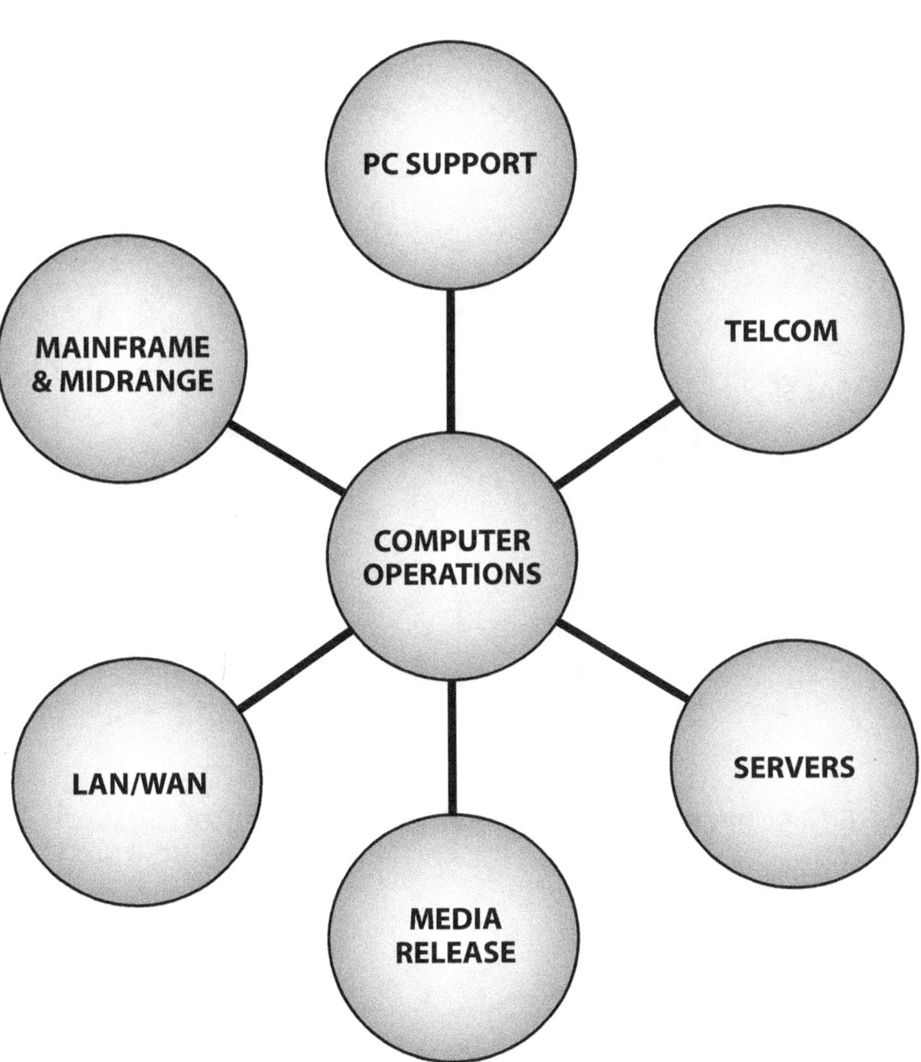

Business Unit Team Chart

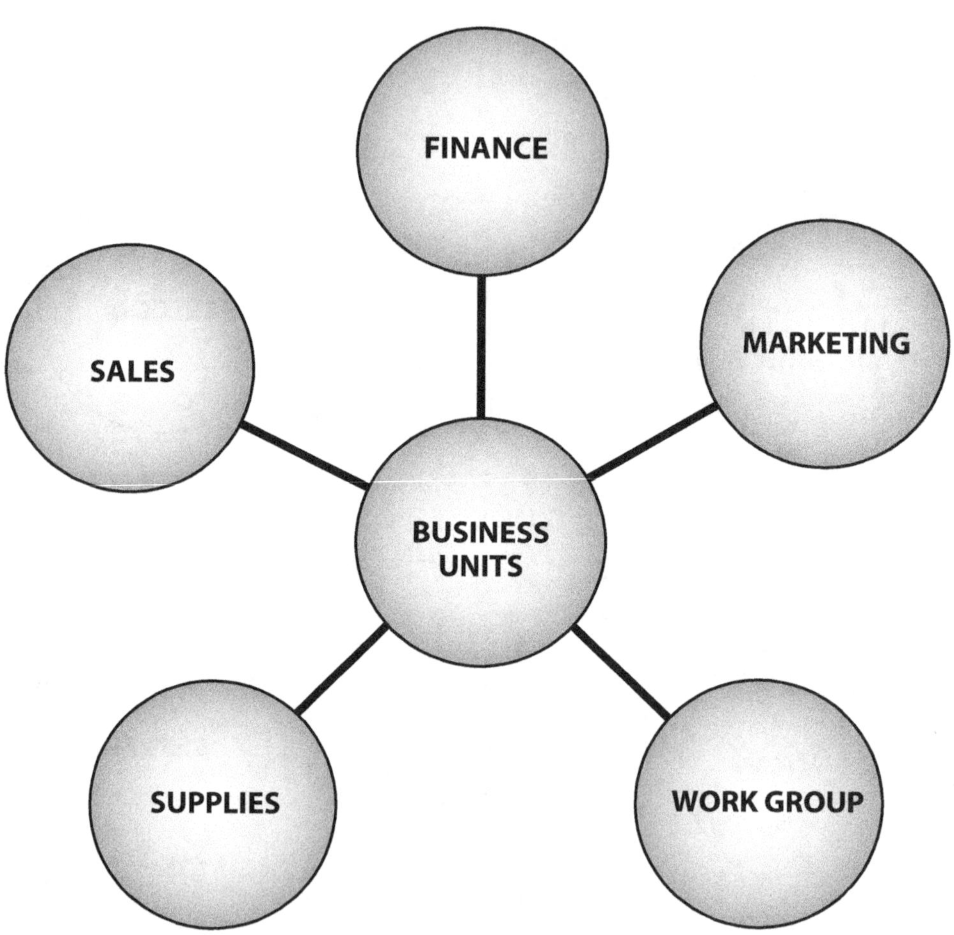

Recovery Logistics Team Chart

Call Response Team Chart

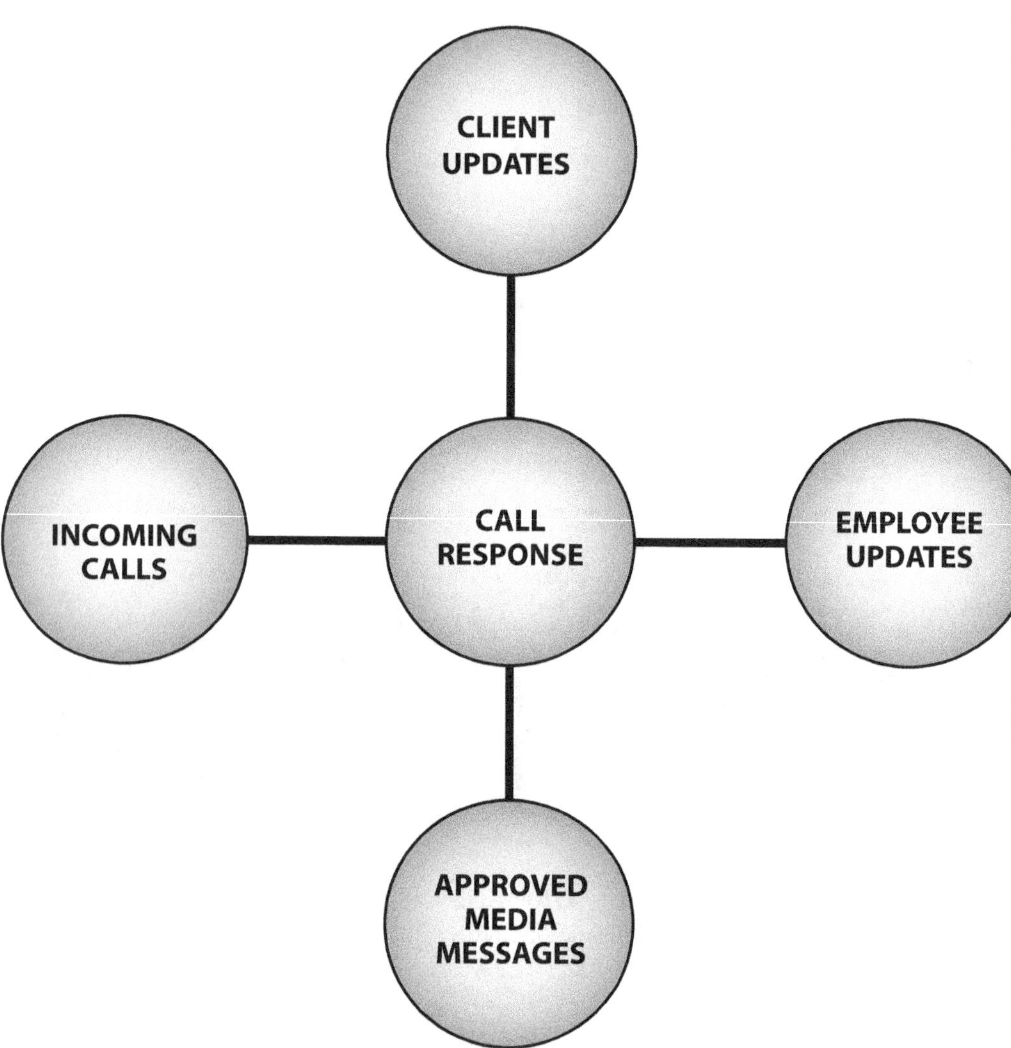

A more fully developed contingency organization would look something like this chart:

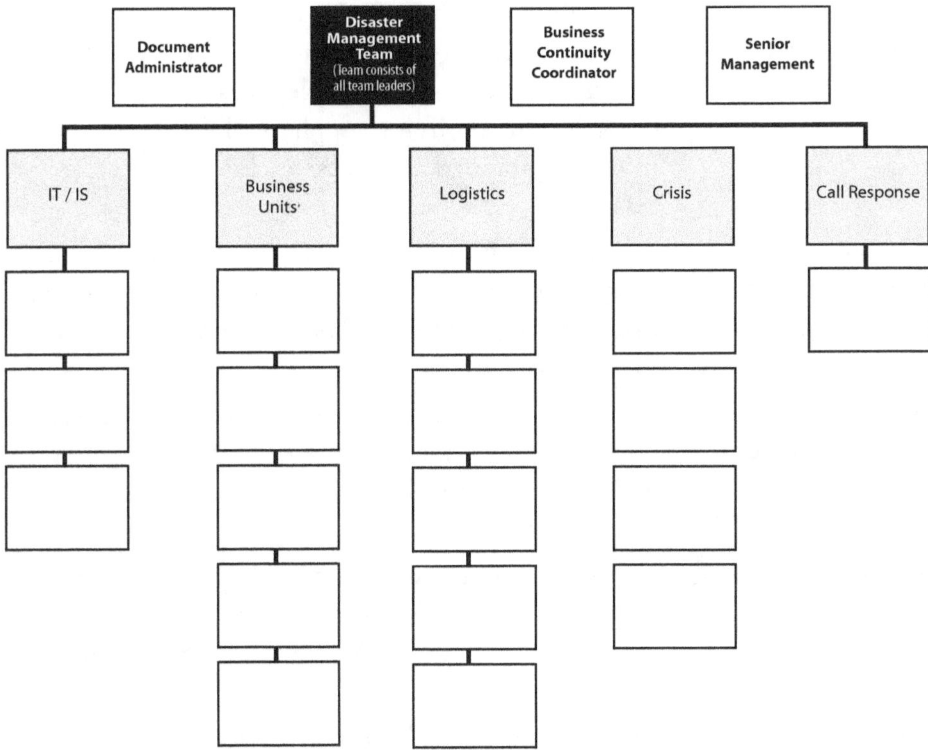

Team Definitions

Team Leaders	Team leaders are responsible for coordinating all of the recovery communications within their sub-teams and between other recovery teams during the recovery process. Good communications among teams and members is essential to speed of response.
Team Tasks	Individual responsibilities must be clearly identified and assigned to specific people on each team. Tasks could include notifying suppliers where to deliver, informing important clients, tracking recovery progress, etc.
Temporary Command Center	A central location selected as a meeting place for a temporary period of time enabling a quick confirmation of recovery personnel notification and confirming the recovery plan.
The Permanent Command Center	After teams have been mobilized, team leaders set up a permanent command center at the recovery site. This is the location where they will coordinate their team efforts.
Recovery	The process of planning for and/or implementing recovery of less time-sensitive business operations and processes after critical business functions have resumed.
Team Template	The form used to collect information that defines the scope, functions, and responsibilities of a BCP team (a sample form is included at the end of this chapter).

Sample Team Leader Responsibilities

The following items represent samples of individual team leader responsibilities/tasks.

- Work closely with other business continuity team leaders to ensure smooth integration of all recovery tasks
- Evaluate and critique initial disaster assessment reports and action plans
- Track the actual progress/completion of recovery activities against the projected sequence of recovery events (i.e., function as a project manager for the recovery process)

- Motivate and direct the members of their teams
- Serve as the prime decision-maker for situations not included in this plan
- Create additional recovery positions as needed to assist in recovery activities
- Submit final disaster assessment reports to the business continuity coordinator
- Assign team members to particular team tasks detailed in the team section of the plan document
- Train team members in their team assignments; this will have a significant impact on the amount of time required to recover

Sample Team Responsibilities and Tasks

Crisis Management

- Maintain general safety and protect the good name of the company
- Ensure safety of all employees at all locations
- Prepare authorized release of information for clients, employees, and media for distribution by the call response team
- Handle emergencies of all types that occur on company property
- Respond to legal issues arising from emergencies
- Counsel employees after traumatic event

Information Technology

- Procure necessary equipment to recover essential IT services needed to recover identified business critical data and software
- Confirm with logistics team that proper IT equipment has been received and site is prepared
- Invoke any appropriate recovery contracts (logistics team will make phone calls for you)
- Install equipment
- Load and test OS
- Load and test applications
- Synchronize data with applications
- Set up and test LAN and WAN
- Test system

- Set up PC workstations
- Modify applications as necessary to synchronize correctly with data

Business Units

- Set up work area and communications system
- Organize your workload immediately in such a way that some or all of it can be carried out without a computer for a period of up to seventy-two hours
- Begin contacting clients to make sure they understand you had a disaster and are working with temporary limitations
- Monitor delivery of their critical documents from disaster site and off-site storage facility to recovery site
- Monitor time-critical job tasks such as file transfers or cash transfers
- Monitor logistics team's success by obtaining any critical documents at the disaster site that your team has identified
- Monitor logistics team's progress by obtaining items your team stored at the off-site storage location
- Follow your task list to make sure you have successfully recovered your unit's essential operations
- As various parts of your business unit become operable, either manually or with computer, begin actual work—limiting this work to essential services only until all of your basic recovery tasks have been completed and you know you will be able to carry out a normal day's activities

Recovery Logistics

- Notify recovery site that a disaster has been declared and ensure preparations are made for arrival of recovery workers
- Notify off-site storage vendor(s), requesting them to deliver disaster recovery items to recovery location
- Provide damage estimates of disaster site
- Invoke IT/IS recovery contracts at the request of the IS team leader
- Assist IT/IS by initiating call to hardware vendor or IT recovery site

- Obtain contract personnel to assist in carrying out the recovery process
- Contact vendors as needed
- Receive request for supplies, food, and equipment from other teams; place those orders, then see that the delivery is sent to the appropriate recovery site
- Function as shipping and receiving department
- Attempt to recover salvageable items from inside damaged facility
- Arrange for transportation of salvageable material, company personnel, contract personnel, purchased goods and materials
- Arrange for lodging as necessary

Call Response

- Distribute authorized updates to employees
- Distribute authorized releases and updates to media
- Distribute authorized releases and updates to clients
- Route calls to appropriate recovery teams when teams are prepared to receive them

When each of these steps has been completed, the next phase of BCP development is completion of the call-down chart. Information for the chart is collected by completing a team template. A sample team template is shown here:

Team Template and Instructions

Instructions

1. Enter your team name
2. Give a brief description of your team's function during recovery
3. List the team responsibilities
4. List the team tasks
5. Provide the name, assigned task, and contact numbers (work, home, cell, pager) for each team member
6. Provide a list of the equipment, supplies, and/or software required at the off-site location and how many of each item (e.g., three desks)
7. Provide a list of the important documents required at the off-site and where the document can be located

Team Name: ____

Team Function: ____

____

Name	Responsibility	Contact Information
	Team Leader	W: H: C: P:
	Team Member	W: H: C: P:
	Team Member	W: H: C: P:

Team Responsibilities

-
-

Team Tasks (First seventy-two hours)

-
-

Team Tasks (After seventy-two hours)

-
-

Equipment/Supplies/Software

Team Name: ______________________________

Equipment	Quantity
PC	
Fax / Copier	
Scanner	
Printer	
Cell Phone / Charger	
Other:	
Supplies	**Quantity**
Desk / Chairs	
Misc. Supplies (paper, pens, pencils, stapler, notebooks, paper	
Other:	
Software	**Quantity**
Dial-up Modem	
Internet Access	
MS Office	
E-mail	
Other:	

Important Documents	**Location**
1. ______________________	______________________
2. ______________________	______________________
3. ______________________	______________________
4. ______________________	______________________

After the teams have been designated and staffed they must be trained to act as emergency recovery teams in addition to their usual functions. The next chapter describes team training.

CHAPTER 7

TEAM TRAINING

Introduction to BCP Training

The primary training objective is to create a mind-set of response. People who know how to do things will do them when they need doing. People who understand why they are doing things will be more likely to do them, even without direction. Good examples are doctors, nurses, firemen, and police, what we commonly call role personnel. They are a product of their training. Disaster recovery personnel are also a product of their training. They will respond quickly because they are trained to do so.

Making the decisions required by disaster quickly depends largely on the quality of information available. The risk assessment process and business impact analysis provide quality information for threat review to enable good recovery decisions rendered promptly.

Risk assessment, business impact analysis, clustering, and recovery team development, reviewed regularly, provide vehicles for increasing awareness of hazards and risks. With this diligence, the organization will be more likely to take sensible precautions. Regular analysis will provide the necessary quality information to create constant adjustment to existing conditions. A bonus effect is reducing the possibility of surprise. Regular repetition of these processes is an effective form of training in itself.

The most significant aspect of training for recovery activities is making certain everyone in the contingency organization has the same knowledge of what has to happen and in what order. Common knowledge and training provide an inventory of capabilities that is the same for everyone. They are designed as protection against duplication of functions when time is of the essence. Common training to the BCP also causes the contingency organization to recognize what is, accept reality, and determine reasonable responses.

The range of responses that comes from analysis and knowledge of the organization's abilities makes planning for response a natural event. Response scenarios can be planned out and exercised. Corrections can be made as necessary to achieve the desired results. The plans can then be rehearsed to the point that all personnel know exactly what to do, and are comfortable in their knowledge that they can accomplish what they set out to do in spite of what adversity might be facing them. This process is called training. There is no substitute for it.

Dimensions of Disaster

The dimensions of disaster are outlined in chapter one. The length of interruption is generally the governing factor. Use the same factor, length of disruption, and apply the information available from risk assessment, business impact analysis, with weather and environment conditions. With this process risk managers are quite capable of predicting the possibility, probability, and likely dimensions of any series of events.

The form for threat review, from chapter two, is designed to capture information from several sources to facilitate maintaining a status board. The concept is for risk managers to advise department heads of existing threats, to which department heads would estimate the probable impact on their activities and personnel. The end result is an impending event notice to which the organization can respond.

For predictable events such as snowstorms, thunderstorms, hurricanes, and floods, it affords protection time. It is also advance notice of what recovery activities might be required. Prompt reaction to advance notice can save literally millions of dollars. The same diligence applied before an unpredictable event can provide very valuable time to prepare recovery.

Another factor of immense value in planning and training is lessons learned. The sources of learning can be quite varied:

Lessons Learned from Disasters

1. Executive leadership is critical
2. Good media relations are a must
3. Need for a command center
4. The importance of vendors
5. Facility security is required
6. Employee safety training
7. *Planning is essential*

Compliance

Compliance with public laws, regulations, industry standards, insurance carrier's demands, and auditors' requirements has become a much more important factor than at any time previously. There are a number of factors that have led to the current state of affairs with compliance. These factors are relevant only in that they point the way to compliance. Compliance generally makes organizations more effective. It also reduces exposure to financial reverses and avoids penalties for noncompliance.

Appendix A is a list of definitions that apply to and further explain compliance. Appendix B is a chart of current laws, regulations, and standards to serve as a guide to determine which standards your organization may be required to meet. It is *not* all inclusive. All organizations should have their legal departments and auditors research and prepare an opinion of what their organization must do to get into and maintain compliance with existing standards. Activities to maintain standards should be included in training plans and schedules.

The Role of Business Impact Analysis (BIA)

The most significant use of business impact analysis is calculating the effect of a severe business interruption and measuring it in dollar amounts. Effective application of BIA requires some special information and the knowledge of how to make use of it. Chapter three describes the process, and provides a form for collecting the significant information needed to determine financial impact. Training will teach the disaster management organization how to interpret the information they have collected. Operating departments, assisted by cost accounting departments can help fulfill this process:

1. Identify core functions by priority—those having the greatest impact on service, revenue, and compliance

2. Determine business impact on these core operations assuming normal support components may be absent or curtailed
3. Calculate the span of time to restore critical IS and IT systems
4. Calculate the span of time to recover time-sensitive business operations
5. Calculate the hourly financial cost based on calculated recovery times

Don't Estimate—Calculate!

Good decisions are dependent on thorough and diligent analysis more than any other factor with the possible exception of good luck. Good luck is more probable when your chances are graced by good, and timely, information. The end result of business impact analysis is a clearly defined recovery strategy.

Clustering

Business unit clustering is a process designed to identify critical business functions that must be recovered first in the event of severe interruption. Training to accomplish effective clustering would include these concepts:

- *Don't try to create recovery teams that match your organizational structure*
- Create recovery teams to systematically *restore* critical business functions

The clustering questionnaire is an important tool for training. It aids in outlining disaster levels. It is an information gathering device for deciding on and developing the contingency organization. Training should include familiarity with the form, the information it seeks, and determining in advance where the information is likely to be found in the quickest manner. This is the portion of the process that forms the single page team plans.

Team Interviewing

Face-to-face questioning is a quick and efficient method of discovering the difference between day-to-day details and emergency action tasks. Business continuity coordinators who conduct these interviews should be guided by their recovery strategy in preparing questions for interview sessions. The sample questions shown in the interviewing chapter and format of team templates can be used to acquire necessary critical information. The purpose of team interviewing is to:

- Meet with representatives of key departments to identify the flow of information
- Identify where information is received, and where it is passed off to others
- Determine information flow frequency (e.g., daily, weekly, monthly)
- Identify critical functions and tasks from communication information
- Create a recovery team structure based on tasks to be accomplished

Training of the BCC and team leaders should include rehearsals of questioning team members and practice in listening to answers to make certain all critical information is recognized.

Team Selection and Organization

Training for team selection and organization processes has several steps that need to be learned so the effort conforms to the BCP model. This information later becomes a single page team plan.

1) Identify team responsibilities
2) Identify tasks required to fulfill those responsibilities
3) List items needed to perform team functions
4) Provide appendixes as appropriate

Each of these steps has characteristics that need to be explained to facilitate their completion:

- Identify core teams
- Identify and interview team leaders
- Configure recovery teams specifically for restoring critical business functions
- Interview team members individually to identify subject matter experts
- Clearly identify team responsibilities and tasks that must be assigned to specific people on each team
- Assign team member tasks
- Decide communication modes and style (Team leaders are responsible for coordinating all of the recovery communications within their sub-teams and between other recovery teams during the recovery process.)

Team Development

Training for team development should generally follow the business continuity model. The structure of the model is designed and operated to create a mindset and culture of being prepared for any eventuality so response to adversity is immediate and quick. Emphasis is pointed toward identifying the necessary. The steps are grouped to show that subsequent functions may be operating simultaneously with others. The first group is the basic structure of the contingency organization. When that phase is complete, the additional groupings will operate in support of the contingency organization. The training objective would have all the members of the contingency organization know and understand each step in the development process.

Development steps and the sequence to follow:

Contingency Organization

1. Identify recovery coordinator
2. Identify critical functions by priority
3. Identify business functions by priority
4. Identify workgroup requirements
5. Designate recovery teams

IS/IT Team

6. Prioritize business critical software by platform
7. Prioritize business critical data
8. Locate business critical documentation
9. Identify server restoration sequence

IS/IT Sub-Team

10. Determine business unit recovery requirements
11. Calculate data restoration time
12. Identify restoration requirements and scripts
13. Calculate length of time to restore hardware
14. Calculate length of time to restore software
15. Calculate length of time to sync data

Recovery Logistics Team

16. Develop off-site storage procedures
17. Create off-site storage inventory
18. Create vendor phone list
19. Create vendor maintenance contract list

Disaster Management Team

20. Identify team leaders by recovery function
21. Train team leaders
22. Identify recovery locations by platform
23. Identify workgroup recovery location by unit

Crisis Management Team

24. Estimate cost of downtime by time and function
25. Identify and train company spokesperson

Within those team development groups there are specific activities to learn and accomplish. Just as the development of the business continuity plan is done in steps, so is the training done in steps that keep the process manageable and facilitate scheduling:

Step One

- Identify business continuity coordinator
- Identify departments
- List critical department functions
- Prioritize functions
- Select team leaders

Step Two

- Identify department recovery tasks
- Identify recovery time requirements
- Prioritize recovery tasks
- Identify department dependencies

Step Three

- Identify subject matter experts
- Determine requirements for off-site storage
- Identify workgroup recovery requirements

Step Four

- Identify application software
- List software by priority/platform
- Identify data files/databases
- List data by priority/platform
- Identify critical/essential data
- List by priority, platform, workgroup
- Document system software
- List servers by priority, location, and dependencies

Step Five

- Identify recovery location(s)
- Determine recovery location by workgroup and department
- Estimate downtime costs by function, departmental unit, and span of time

Step Six

- Document all restore procedures for each department
- Identify essential services restoration requirements
- Identify specific documents required to conduct essential business
- Identify IT downtime tolerance
- Calculate time to restore and sync data

Step Seven

- Identify off-site storage procedures
- Identify off-site storage inventory
- Obtain vendor list and phone numbers
- Gather vendor maintenance contract information
- Obtain employee phone list

Step Eight

- Finalize plan document
- Identify document maintenance and control
- Schedule recovery exercises
- Conduct training exercise
- Evaluate training exercise

Team responsibilities applicable to all teams:
Develop single-page team plans.

- Select team leader
- Select team members
- Identify team responsibilities
- Identify tasks required to fulfill those responsibilities
- List items needed to perform team functions
- Provide appendix as appropriate
- Identify essential documents and their locations.

REMEMBER

The primary recovery objective is to identify what needs to be accomplished immediately after a disaster.

Training

The first step in training is committing to doing it. The previous pages in this chapter have described all the information needed to formulate a training program. Many of the sequences required are also noted. A training regimen should start with information required for individuals to elevate their competencies. Next is sub-team training, then team training. The last step would be combined exercises. The progressive nature of the training levels is creating a series of successful repetitions.

When your program design is complete, calculate the amount of time needed for each level of training, and the resources needed to sustain the program. Match your training schedule to your business continuity plan to ensure that you are creating the skills to execute the plan.

Create a project training schedule and stick to it.

There is one significant training objective:

Train Your Teams To Recover!

An important aspect of emergency response training is that contingency organization meetings and training sessions require all team leaders and team members of all recovery teams to be present. Each team must clearly understand the activities for which their team, and all other teams are responsible, so that no activity is duplicated during an actual disaster and all required tasks are completed.

Each team then meets separately and assigns specific responsibilities and tasks to each individual team member. It is the responsibility of all team leaders to update their single page team plans and to make sure all of their team members understand and are able to carry out assigned tasks and responsibilities.

Communications

The importance of effective communications cannot be overstated. The system and style of communications between BCC and team leaders and team members must be consistent and quick. It requires communications discipline (listening constantly, speaking only when necessary) to ensure that nets are kept open.

An orderly and clearly defined call up process should be put in place.

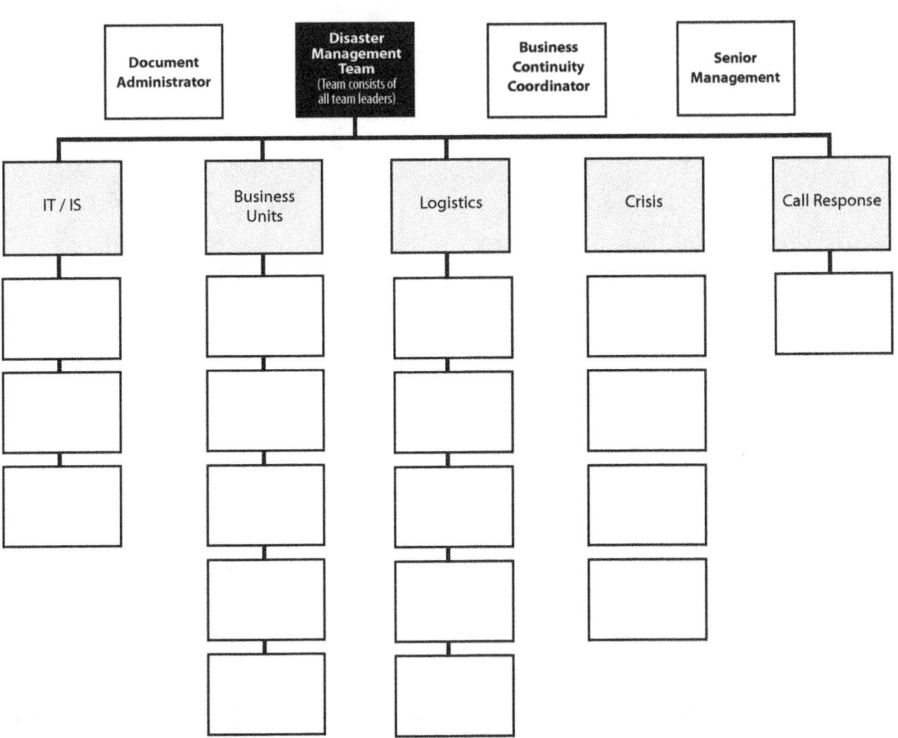

There are several steps that will lead to establishing a standard mode and style for communications within the contingency organization:

- Meet with representatives of key departments to identify the flow of information
- Identify where information is received, and where it is passed off to others
- Determine information flow frequency (e.g., daily, weekly, monthly)

This chapter has dealt more with the training of individuals and teams. This effort is designed to prepare the contingency organization for the exercises described in chapter 9. The next chapter describes the business continuity plan document, which later serves as a guidebook.

CHAPTER 8

RECOVERY PLAN DOCUMENT

Description of a Recovery Plan Document

The recovery plan document is a printed version of the recovery plan. In general, the recovery plan should expect the worst case. It should provide instructions and information on what to do including essential details on procedures, directions, and schedules.

Create your recovery plan document using a standard word processing program in order to simplify document maintenance. There are several benefits you should expect:

- Provide for orderly recovery
- Reduce the length of business interruption
- Identify core business functions
- Identify key team members
- Document recovery tasks
- Reduce litigation risks
- Reduce compliance issues

A completed disaster recovery plan can reduce critical business recovery time from weeks to just hours—and often reduce your business interruption insurance premiums by up to 20 percent.

Create Your Recovery Plan and Training To Satisfy:

- Auditors and Regulators
- IRS rulings
- Clients
- Employees
- Investors

Elements of a Business Continuity Plan

1. *Identify core requirements*
2. *Identify emergency tasks*
3. *Identify key team members*
4. *Create plan document*
5. *Create appropriate training*
6. *Conduct training exercise*
7. *Document training exercise*

How to Use the Document

1. To learn about the issues involved in planning for the continuity of the critical and essential functions associated with the company's core operations
2. As a checklist of preparation tasks
3. To train personnel and to exercise teams
4. To recover from an actual disaster

Why Is The Business Recovery Plan Document Important?

The recovery plan document is the best evidence of the effort to prepare for a disrupting event. While large organizations—because of their size, complexity, and range of risks—generally have more to lose and more ways to lose what they have than smaller organizations, smaller firms often suffer the most devastating results from seemingly minor business interruptions. Smaller size imposes stricter limits on the ability of an organization to absorb losses and respond to interruptions. The recovery plan is the means to minimizing the effects of disaster.

The recovery plan is in a constant state of change; it evolves as company technology evolves and as personnel responsibilities change. If any part of the document requires change, those changes should be made as soon as current information is available and confirmed.

A documented business continuity plan should meet all the organization's auditing requirements. Its contents should reference the purpose of the document and describe the training processes used to ensure the organization's ability to recover from disaster. To be effective, it must be kept up to date.

When Should It Be Completed?

A business continuity plan is *never* a finished document—it evolves as business changes and improves over time.

It is not expected to be *perfect* or *complete* at any point in time.

Document Control

The document administrator exercises control over the publication and distribution of the printed business continuity plan. This control would include numbering all copies and requiring individuals to sign for a copy to ensure positive control.

Procedure changes, modifications, and updates to the plan are expected and should be organized in the following manner:

- Notify plan administrator when changes are made
- Update the plan on a regular basis
- Maintain and update the teams portion of the plan
- Track changes to the plan in a designated section of the plan
    - (i) Indicate page number on which change occurs
    - (ii) Describe change(s)
    - (iii) Note date change(s) was made
- The plan administrator will reprint the document when appropriate
- The plan administrator will complete a new document maintenance log when a new version of the document is printed

- Distribute updates to individuals assigned copies of the plan
- Follow company control procedures

Remember it is the *training* that restores services–not the document.

NOTE: The recovery plan document is not intended to be a procedure manual that covers all departmental functions. It includes only those high priority tasks required to ensure recovery of essential operations after a disaster.

Documentation Tasks

- Make changes directly on the pages of the plan that require change
- Track those changes in the appendix of the document
- Indicate the page number on which the change occurs
- Describe the change
- Note the date the change was made
- Indicate the date the change notification was made to document administrator
- Document administrator makes changes in the master document
- Document administrator notes changes and team names in the appendix of the master document
- Teams notify document administrator of all changes when changes are made
- Reprint the document when appropriate
- Complete the document maintenance log when a new version of the document is printed
- Distribute updates to those individuals assigned copies of the plan

Documentation Tasks (continued)

- Follow company document control procedures
- Determine the number of copies of the plan that are necessary
- Assign document control numbers to the plan copies
- Distribute completed copies of the plan to the team leaders and appropriate team members
- Distribute updated copies of the plan at least annually
- Issue plan updates by replacing complete plans
- Account for all previous copies of the plan and then destroy them
- Reassign plan copies if employees with team leader or backup responsibilities leave the organization or their responsibilities change
- Require return of the plan copy whenever an employee is terminated

Document Layout

The business continuity plan should include, but is not limited to the following sections:

Examples of information pertinent to the plan follow on the next few pages.

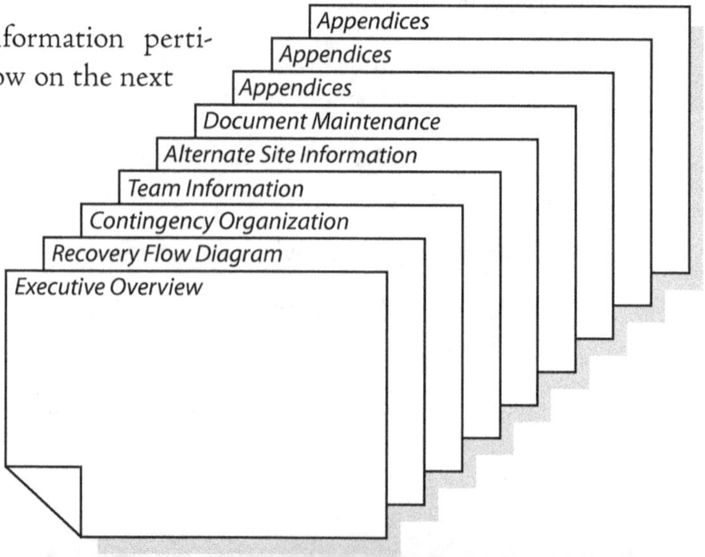

Sample Recovery Site Information

XYZ Corporation
7890 Some River Drive
Anywhere, MN 55400

Services Available At Alternate Site

- Private office
- Baby-sitting or child care
- Security on-site
- Secretarial services
- Accessible to wheelchairs
- Photocopy service
- Internet access
- Fax
- Elevators
- Business center
- Parking area patrolled
- Post/Parcel service
- Computer use available
- A-V equipment rental

Sample Equipment/Supplies/Software Checklist

	EQUIPMENT / SUPPLIES / SOFTWARE																			
	PC	Typewriter	Calculator	Fax / Paper	Copier / Paper	Scanner	Ink Jet Printers	Laser Printer	Telephones	Cell Phones	Radio (Battery)	Camera	Cassette Recorder	Desks / Chairs	Misc. Office Supplies *	Dial-up Modem	Internet Access	MS Office	Email	*See individual team lists*
IS Team																				
Desktop																				
Network Svcs																				
Servers																				
Telephony																				
Business Units																				
Human Resources																				
Finance																				
Sales																				
Supply Chain																				
Crisis Management																				
Corporate Comm.																				
Comp/Benefits																				
Health/Safety																				
Security																				
Legal																				
Logistics																				
Travel																				
Records Mgmt																				
Childcare																				
Damage Asmt/ Salvage																				
Recovery Site Mobil.																				
Call Team																				
Consumer Calls																				
Customer Calls																				
Employee Calls																				
TOTAL																				

* Miscellaneous Office Supplies: paper, pens, pencils, stapler, paper clips, tape, notebooks.

Appendix Checklist

Name	Description
Documentation Inventory	Contains a list of all documentation required for recovery and the location where that documentation is stored.
BCP Exercise Schedule and Report	Contains information about disaster recovery review exercises that have taken place using the plan.
Alternate Site Information	Contains information about the alternate recovery site, including address, phone, services, etc.
Employee Phone List	Contains contact information for employees during the recovery.
Floor Plans	Contains photos/diagrams of company floor plans.
Hardware/Software Information	Contains pertinent hardware/software information required during a recovery.
Main-frame Specific Information	Contains information necessary to recover the mainframe (i.e., hardware/software inventory for mainframe).
Misc. Team Information	Contains team information not team-specific required during the recovery.
Network Diagrams	Contains diagrams of the current company network.
Network-Specific Information	Contains information necessary to recover the network.
Off-site Storage Information	Contains information about current off-site storage (i.e., a list of all documents, disks, tapes, etc.)
Recovery Contact Log	Contains emergency contact information.

Name	Description
Regional Information	Contains information about the local community (i.e., hotels, ground services, courier services, etc.)
Server Restore Time Estimate	Contains estimated recovery times and costs under emergency conditions.
Server-specific Information	Contains information necessary to recover critical servers and recovery times.
Telecom Information	Contains information necessary to recover telecommunications.
Transmission-Specific Information	Contains information necessary to recover transmissions.
Vendor Information	Contains a listing of all vendors of hardware, software, and other necessary supplies/services used.
Notes	Provides an area for any additional notes/information.

Sample Recovery Checklist

Use the following checklist to identify that specific actions have occurred and note the day and time the action occurred. Note: All items may not be required depending on the type of disaster.

	ACTIVITY	TIME: *Day and Hour*
1	Who reported the disaster?	
	Name: ______	
	Job Assignment: ______	
2	Disaster management team members notified:	______
	BCP administrator	______
	Facilities team leader	______
	Hardware/Applications team leader	______
	Data recovery team leader	______
	Logistics team leader	______
	Damage assessment team leader	______
	Crisis management team leader	______
	Vendor contact team leader	______
	Communications team leader	______
	Customer response team leader	______
3	Initial damage assessment?	______
4	Disaster level declared? (1, 2, 3)	______
5	Business continuity plan activated	______
6	Senior management notified	______
7	Team member notifications initiated	______
8	Alternate site activated	______

	ACTIVITY	TIME: *Day and Hour*
9	Critical business requirements confirmed	______
10	Recovery team members:	______
	IT recovery team is at recovery site	______
	Critical software restored	______
	Critical production reestablished	______
	Telecommunications reestablished	______
	Alternate site operational	______
11	Meet with BCP administrative and other team personnel as necessary	______
12	Senior management status updates made	______
	Status #1	______
	Status #2	______
	Status #3	______
13	Team leaders review recovery checklist with team members	______
14	Suggested plan changes for improvement	______
15	All BCP team members notified	______
16	BCP team members reported in	______
17	Begin damage assessment	______
18	All team managers assembled	______
19	Plan activated	______
20	Control center activated	______
21	Vendor contracts invoked	______
22	Off-site storage vendor notified	______

ACTIVITY	TIME: *Day and Hour*
23 All team leaders at control center	______
24 Alternate site accepted notification and is standing by	______
25 Recovery teams:	______
Team members arrived at recovery site	______
Transportation requirements confirmed by logistics	______
Tapes dispatched to alternate site	______
Records sent to alternate site	______
Salvaged data/documents identified	______
Reported to command center	______
Critical systems reload completed/verified/tested	______
Backup communications network established	______
Data communications network tested	______
Basic environment established	______
Systems teams advised of time dependent applications to be reloaded	______
Data verified	______
System teams confirm systems are useable	______
System(s) available to users	______

Sample Floor Plan

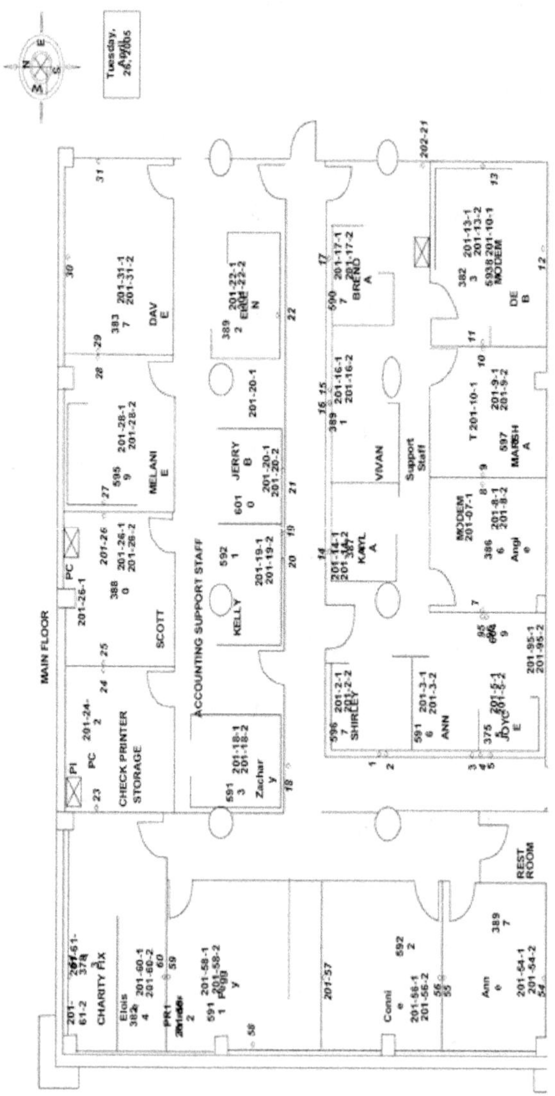

Sample Server Restore Dependency List

Restore Order	Server Name	Restore Time	Dependency
1	AS400	10.8	
2	XYZ	2	
3	Linux Print Server	2	2
4	Uncle	6	4
5	Linux Mail Server	5	
6	NT Server	3	
7	Mail Monitor PC	3	6
8	Mail Backup Server	2	6
9	Test Server	2	
10			
11			
12			
13			
14			
15			
16			
17			
18			
19			
20			

Sample Team Template

See additional samples in appendix G.

Sub-Team: Network Administration

The Network Administration Sub-Team function is to recover business critical computer infrastructure and functionality.

Contact Information

Name	Responsibility	Contact Information
	Team Leader	W. H: C: P:
	Team Member	W: H: C: P:
	Team Member	W: H: C: P:

Team Responsibilities

- Recovery of network servers
- Recovery of LAN and intranet infrastructure

Team Tasks

- Rebuild network servers
- Rebuild network infrastructure (See appendix ____ for details)
- Restore programs, data, and user access as necessary

Equipment/Supplies Required

- Netware manuals
- Tape backup reports
- NT manuals

- Cisco manuals
- Veritas manuals

Important Documents and Location

- Off-site storage–Box #ABC-123
- Off-site storage–Box #DEF-456

CHAPTER 9

PLANNING THE EXERCISE

Exercise Definition

The exercise is a rehearsal of what to do if a disrupting event strikes your organization. It is a practice run of the business continuity plan.

Training is learning how to do designated tasks. Once learned, tasks should be practiced to improve competence, confidence, and speed. After individual and small unit activities have been mastered, a combined exercise should be conducted to work all the small units simultaneously. This combined exercise will help identify any omissions in the plan and where improvements can be made.

Why Is It Important?

Conducting periodic planned exercises is critical. Reasons include:

1 Determine the feasibility of the business continuity process
2 Verify the compatibility of backup facilities
3 Identify deficiencies in existing procedures
4 Identify areas in the plan that require modification or enhancement
5 Provide training to the team leaders and team members

6 Ensure the effectiveness of the various teams involved in the recovery process
7 Demonstrate the ability of the department to recover
8 Provide a mechanism to maintain and update the plan

Who Does It?

The executive management orders the combined exercise. The entire contingency organization participates as directed in their BC manual.

It is the responsibility of all team leaders to update their team plans and advise the BCC and document administrator of the changes. They must also make sure all of their team members know and understand any changes that have been made, and are able to carry out their assigned responsibilities.

When Should It Be Done?

A combined exercise should be planned and executed as soon as practicable after designation of a contingency organization. Team training should be conducted before scheduling a combined exercise. Initially, exercises should not be scheduled at critical points in the normal processing cycle. The duration of the exercises should be predetermined to measure response time. Adequate time must be scheduled for review after the exercises are completed.

Exercise Structure

The exercises to be conducted correspond directly to the different severity levels defined. Each planned exercise will be comprised of the following:

- Scenario description
- Assumptions
- Personnel to be involved
- Guidelines and procedures
- External observer(s)
- Documented results
- Post-exercise review and critique meetings
- Management signature(s)
- Rotating staff

In order to properly test notification procedures, business impact, off-site procedures, and recovery site procedures, tests should be conducted during both normal and non-business hours.

All recovery team members should be involved in team exercises. Exercise procedures should be formulated, tested, and documented by the business continuity coordinator prior to the actual exercise.

Conducting Team Exercises

Considerations for developing exercise plans

The management team determines policies to establish the need and frequency for evaluating the plan. They also identify exercise strategies for developing a detailed exercise plan so that, over a period of time, all aspects of the plan can be fully reviewed.

Exercise plans should identify the scope, objectives, and format of the exercise. These exercise plans should be reviewed quarterly.

Review schedule

Training and exercises are performed regularly as needed to support a combined exercise once every twelve months. All team leaders are responsible for the training and training schedules of their teams so their teams are prepared for full department training exercises. In addition, all team leaders are responsible for notifying the plan coordinator when significant changes occur in their areas of responsibility. These changes require updates to the business continuity plan. The updated material is forwarded to the plan coordinator and document administrator prior to any scheduled training exercises.

The objectives of the exercises include:

- Confirmation that the procedures work
- Identification of areas requiring modification
- Rehearsal of procedures and training for personnel
- Increased confidence in the ability of the organization to recover in a timely manner
- Increased speed of response and execution of assigned tasks

Exercise results

The recovery management team documents and reviews the results of the business continuity plan exercises. These results are then presented to senior management for review and made available for audits.

Types of Exercises

Checklist Exercise

A checklist exercise determines whether adequate supplies are stored at the backup site, telephone number listings are current, quantities of forms are adequate, and a copy of the recovery plan and the necessary operating manuals are available. Under this exercising technique, the recovery team reviews the plan and identifies essential components required to be current and available. The checklist exercise ensures this requirement is met.

Table Top Exercise

An exercise to simulate acquisition of information in a disaster situation:

- A recovery team is assembled around a table
- A structured scenario is established
- At timed intervals, messages are fed to team members who generate specific responses
- Team members describe their responses
- Frequency of messages and urgency required is increased to simulate increasing tensions

Structured Conference Room Walk-through Disaster Simulation Exercise

During a structured conference room walk-through disaster simulation exercise, business continuity team members meet to verbally walk through the specific steps of each component of the business continuity process as documented in the business continuity plan. The purpose of the structured walk-through exercise is to confirm the effectiveness of the plan and to identify gaps, bottlenecks, or other plan weaknesses.

Initially, a combination of the checklist and structured walk-through exercises is suggested to determine modifications to the plan prior to more extensive review.

Simulation Exercise

During this exercise, the organization simulates a disaster during non-business hours so normal operations are not interrupted. A disaster scenario identifies the following:

- Purpose of the exercise
- Assumptions

- Objectives
- Type of exercise
- Timing
- Scheduling
- Duration
- Exercise participants
- Assignments
- Constraints
- Exercise steps
- Review and critique

Performing a review exercise can include notification procedures, temporary operating procedures, and backup and recovery operations. During a simulation, the following elements are evaluated:

- Hardware
- Software
- Personnel
- Data and voice communications
- Procedures
- Supplies and forms
- Documentation
- Transportation
- Utilities (power, air conditioning, heating, ventilation)
- Recovery site processing

Parallel Exercise

A parallel review exercise can be performed in conjunction with the checklist review or simulation exercise. Under this scenario, historical transactions, such as the previous day's transactions, are processed by using the preceding day's backup files at the contingency processing site or recovery site. All reports produced at the recovery site by using the backup files must agree with those reports produced at the normal processing site.

Full-interruption Exercise

A full-interruption exercise activates the total business continuity plan. This exercise is costly and could disrupt normal operations, and therefore, must be approached with caution.

Sample Team Training Exercise Agenda

1. Review disaster definitions
2. Recovery team overview
3. How to update the document
4. Whiteboard walk-through
5. Document walk-through
6. Video to demonstrate a recovery
7. Training exercise
8. Exercise review and wrap-up

Recovery planning and training will reduce critical recovery time from weeks to just hours.

Chapter Summary

A complete business continuity plan and appropriate training will:

- Provide for an orderly recovery
- Reduce services interruption
- Identify core functions
- Identify key team members
- Document recovery tasks
- Reduce litigation risks

An important aspect of team training and contingency organization exercises is revealing plan inadequacies and missing elements. These are called gaps. The next chapter describes gap analysis.

CHAPTER 10

CONDUCTING A GAP ANALYSIS

Identifying and Closing Gaps in Business Continuity Plans

After the baseline plan has been established, the plan should be analyzed for any omissions or inadequacies. This is known as a Gap Analysis. Gap analysis is normally done in the final phase of the business continuity plan. It is the first step in continuous improvement of the plan. The first gap analysis should be performed by auditors or experienced managers with BCP training and expertise, thorough knowledge of the organization and its properties and operations. Once the gaps have been identified, they must be eliminated or closed. Executive management and the BCC should take action to assign accountability for each area in question and direct action to correct the gaps.

As you perform a gap analysis, fill out a report card using the forms on the following pages. One is for describing the operational gaps, the other is for describing the information missing from your written plan.

Continuous improvement of the BCP is an essential element of the plan. This phase should also include enhancements, ongoing maintenance, and streamlining of the plan. In addition, exercises should be scheduled in regular sequences in order to establish business continuity rehearsals as a regular business rhythm. By setting up a schedule and establishing a regular business rhythm, you will ensure the business continuity plan will always include up-to-date information.

A governance structure should be established to drive plan accountability and ensure that roles and responsibilities are clearly stated and the BCP sticks to only that which is necessary. This structure should also function to ingrain response and preparedness in the company culture.

The next sequence, What to Do Immediately After a Disaster, describes a basic BCP scenario that includes all of the essential elements of a BCP standard plan. A comparison of your plan to this would show any immediate gaps. This comparison is an example of the diligence and attention to detail required to make an effective gap analysis.

What to Do Immediately After a Disaster

Disaster Management Team

- Business continuity coordinator (BCC) notified of interrupting event
- BCC declares disaster
- BCC notifies executive management and identifies level of disaster
- BCC activates business continuity plan by contacting a team leader
- Team leader notified by BCC contacts all other team leaders

Recovery Teams

- Team leaders alert their team members and request them to stay where they are until further contact
- Damage and assessment team members immediately report to damaged facility to assess damage and report findings to disaster management team

Recovery Logistics Team

- Logistics team notifies recovery site that plan has been activated

Disaster Management Team

- Team leaders assemble at command center forming recovery management team
- Team leaders confirm team member notification with BCC

- Management team confirms disaster level
- Recovery plan goal is to recover essential services within seventy-two hours
- Team leaders re-contact their team members directing them to begin recovery operations at the recovery site
- Team members provide updates to their team leaders on a timely basis
- Logistics team notifies off-site storage vendor to deliver recovery materials

Call Response Team

- Call response team sets up and activates call center

Crisis Management Team

- HR sub-team accounts for all personnel
- Crisis management team (HR and Safety/Security sub-teams) monitors recovery workers checking for abnormal behavior
- Security is established at the damaged site, recovery site, and the command center
- Logistics team tracks outgoing vendor requests, incoming materials, and contract personnel

IS/IT Team

- Confirms with logistics team that proper IT equipment has been received and site is prepared
- Installs equipment
- Loads and tests OS
- Loads and tests applications
- Synchronizes data with applications
- Sets up and tests LAN and WAN
- Sets up PC workstations

Business Unit Teams

- Monitor delivery of their critical documents from disaster site and off-site storage facility to recovery site
- Monitor time-critical job tasks such as file transfers or cash transfers

- Set up work area
- Begin contacting clients, suppliers, and vendors with approved message
- Initiate prioritized list of non-computer dependent duties (begin actual work functions that are designated as essential)

Recovery Logistics Team

- Notifies recovery site that a disaster has been declared and ensures preparations are made for arrival of recovery workers
- Notifies off-site storage vendor requesting them to deliver disaster recovery items to recovery location
- Processes requests from other teams for supplies, food, and equipment
- Contacts vendors as needed
- Invokes IS recovery contracts at the request of the IS team leader
- Functions as shipping and receiving department
- Provides damage estimates of disaster site
- Attempts to recover salvageable items
- Obtains contract personnel to assist in carrying out the recovery process
- Arranges transportation for:
  - Salvageable material
  - Contract personnel
  - Purchased goods and materials
  - Arranges for lodging as necessary

Crisis Management Team

- Releases authorized updates to employees
- Releases authorized updates to media
- Releases authorized updates to clients
- Routes calls to appropriate recovery team when teams are prepared to receive them
- Prepares authorized release of information for clients, employees, and media
- Ensures safety of all employees at all locations
- Handles emergencies of all types that occur on company property

- Responds to legal issues arising from emergencies
- Counsels employees after traumatic event
- Stabilize

When your plan is complete, compare it to the sequences listed above. The differences from your plan and the sequences noted above are gaps, a display of the difference between where you are in your planning and where you want to be. From this initial gap analysis you make changes until your plan does what you need it to do.

Finally, the plan should be ingrained into the organizational culture. This is only possible when senior management has demonstrated ongoing support and can only happen if the business continuity coordinator has effectively championed the business continuity plan into a sustainable long-term plan.

Sample Gap Analysis and Scorecard

Use the following sample scorecard to assist in the identification of gaps in the BC plan.

<table>
<tr><th></th><th>Current Status</th><th>Progress Status</th><th>Headlines & Highlights</th></tr>
<tr><td colspan="3">Infrastructure</td><td rowspan="5">• Program support and executive communications appears to be strong. It is recommended to increase communications at the executive level to ensure awareness is high at that level.
• Command center established at alternate sites. Connectivity expected for all team leads, however specific work station assignments are unclear.
• We recommend a credentialing program that will establish a registered badge for all business continuity team members.
• Voice networking and PC availability will not be pre-planned at the alternate sites.</td></tr>
<tr><td>• Program Sponsor and Communication</td><td>○</td><td>○</td></tr>
<tr><td>• Command Center and Infrastructure</td><td>▽</td><td>○</td></tr>
<tr><td>• Credentialing</td><td>⬣</td><td>▽</td></tr>
<tr><td>• Secure PC availability and related Voice Networking</td><td>⬣</td><td>▽</td></tr>
</table>

	Current Status	Progress Status	Headlines & Highlights
Planned Exercises			• Since the business continuity plan has not been updated since 20XX, it is unclear if exercises have been executed. Plan on developing and executing a conference room structured disaster simulation in 20XX.
• Spring 20XX			
• Fall/winter 20XX			

Plan Documentation – Maintenance and Enhancements			
• IT			• It appears that overall support from the majority of teams continues to be strong. Set up a regular business rhythm that will ensure compliance to proper business continuity guidance. • With the exception of the IT disaster recovery plan, all teams have not updated the BCP. Establish a regular update process that will ensure compliance to the plan.
• Business Units			
• Crisis Management			
• Customer Response			
• Logistics Support			
• Damage Assess. and Salvage			
• Facilities Recovery			

Recommended Enhancements To The Plan			
• Automated Notification System			• We recommend enhancement to the current plan by the addition of an automatic notification and incident management system • Recommend backups of all key contingency team members and team leaders.
• Clearer Plans for Longer Term Recovery Site			
• Develop All Major Communication Scripts			

Legend:	
○	Meets or exceeds minimum requirements.
▽	Meets minimum requirements; however, improvements or additional action needed.
⬣	Changes are necessary.

Business Continuity Document Gap Analysis & Scorecard

	Section	Description	Page#
	IT	**Suggested Refinements**	
▽	Computer Recovery	Need to add hardware/software/ equipment and important documents/location	26
▽	Infrastructure Recovery	Need to add hardware/software/ equipment and important documents/location	28
▽	Application Recovery	Need to add hardware/software/ equipment and important documents/location	31
▽	Data Mgmt	Need to add hardware/software/ equipment and important documents/location	33
	BUSINESS UNITS		
⬣	Team Leaders	Need to identify backups to team leaders	36, 46, 55
⬣	Service and Licensing	Need to identify backup to team leader	60
	CRISIS MANAGEMENT		
▽	Crisis Management	Need to add responsibilities/tasks, hardware/ software/ equipment and important documents/location	65
▽	Legal	Need to add tasks	71
⬣	Workstations	Need to identify backup to team leader	78
	CALL RESPONSE		
▽	Internal IT	Need to identify hardware/ software/equipment	83

	Section	Description	Page#
	IT	Suggested Refinements	
	Internal Information	Need to identify backup to team leader	84
	APPENDIX ITEMS		
	Appendix A	Documentation inventory should contain a listing of all team documentation and its location	95
▽	Appendix B	Update phone listings	96
▽	Appendix D	Update exercise schedule if activity has taken place	122
▽	Appendix M	Identify off-site storage procedures for retrieval of information	177

Continuous Improvement

Continuous improvement for the business continuity plan should include the following:

- **Gap analysis**
- **Ongoing maintenance**
- **Streamlining and enhancements**
- **Establish plan exercises**
- **Establish governance structure**
- **Create a business rhythm**
- **Ingrain in the culture of the company**

After the plan is developed, put in place, and exercised, the next step is deciding on a framework for the future. The next chapter, Going Forward, addresses that issue.

CHAPTER 11

GOING FORWARD

Framework for the Future

The effort expended in the process of planning for emergency recovery or business continuity virtually demands a greater effort to maintain the state of preparedness you have developed in your planning and training. Said simply, don't waste all that effort.

Even though the contingency organization is a smaller and intensely trained group, the scope of disaster effects on your organization should make it obvious that paying attention to possibilities is every employee's job.

There are two factors that should always be at work: **vigilance** and **diligence.**

Vigilance includes constant and consistent application of good security and surveillance measures. It includes good maintenance and good housekeeping. It includes paying attention to long-range and short-term weather reports. It includes being aware of trends in crime and civil disturbance. It includes being aware of Homeland Security hazard levels and states of readiness. It means a constant level of awareness and knowledge of threats and timely reviews of how you and your organization are planning to respond to whatever might happen.

Diligence includes everyday application of good management practices. It includes regularly making changes to your plans to allow for changes of personnel and adapting to changing technology. It means following through to make certain your emergency recovery supplies and equipment are serviceable, in the proper quantities, and in the right places. It includes regular review of communications systems and devices to make certain your organization can communicate effectively with local law and public safety organizations. It means regular training and retraining of first responders to crisis conditions.

What might seem to be buzzwords for a current craze in the business world are actually realistic goals for coping with the emerging state of the world. The new corporate culture is a mind-set of seeing the world as it is because that's the world in which you have to live and operate. Establishing a business rhythm is another way of saying establish a schedule of training for recovery to hone the skills of first responder personnel and repeat the schedule and training regularly.

Response! Planning and Training for Emergency Recovery shows that business continuity can be assured by any organization that sets out to do so. Success in business continuity is most often a combination of two factors:

VIGILANCE and DILIGENCE

APPENDIX A

Compliance Definitions, Standards, and Laws

This list of definitions, standards, and laws is intended as a guide to help organizations decide how to achieve compliance. It is not all inclusive. It is not intended to substitute for legal and audit opinions and should not be construed to do so.

SAS 55 Statement of Auditing Standards Consideration of internal control in a financial statement audit, amended by SAS No. 78, requires an understanding of internal control that reasonably assures: the identification of types of potential misstatements related to assertions, the consideration of factors that affect the risk that misstatements could be material to the financial statements, and the design of appropriate substantive tests.

SAS 70 Statement of Auditing Standards The authoritative guidance that permits service organizations to disclose their control activities and processes to their customers and their customers' auditors in a uniform reporting format. An SAS 70 examination signifies that a service organization has had its control objectives and control activities examined by an independent accounting and auditing firm. A formal report including the auditor's opinion (Service Auditor's Report) is issued to the service organization at the conclusion of an SAS 70 examination.

SAS 78—SAS No. 78 amends SAS No. 55 Replacing its definition and description of the internal control structure with that contained in the COSO report.[3] In addition to a change in the definition of internal control, this change will now require auditors to gain an understanding of five components of internal control rather than the previous three elements. It includes an explanation of these changes together with guidance on how auditors gain and document this new understanding.

[3]Establishes a common framework for an organization's internal control over the areas of operations, financial reporting, and compliance with laws and regulations.

HIPAA Health Insurance Portability and Accountability Act of 1996	Amends the Internal Revenue Code of 1986 to improve portability and continuity of health insurance coverage in the group and individual markets to combat waste, fraud, and abuse in health insurance and health care delivery; to promote the use of medical savings accounts; to improve access to long-term care services and coverage; to simplify the administration of health insurance; and for other purposes. It also includes contingency plan requirements.

Foreign Corrupt Practices Act of 1977 Requirements:

Areas of potential liability are:

- Failure to have an operations contingency plan
- Failure to implement a security program

Liability depends on whether the recovery plan and its implementation were reasonable.

Sarbanes–Oxley Act of 2002

Requires corporations to have good financial controls, especially IT, with business continuity measures effective and audited regularly.

7 CFR Part 1730 Electric System Emergency Restoration Plan

Rural Utilities Service, USDA regulations require electric program distribution, generation, and transmission borrowers to create or expand existing Emergency Restoration Plans to include emergency recovery from natural or man-made disasters. (The Federal Register notice includes extensive detail about what must be included in plans.)

NASD Rules 3510 and 3520

Require business continuity plans for securities companies and emergency contact information.

Rulings and Standards

ISO17799 The Code of Practice for IT Security Management

Violations of SEC regulations mandating standards may result in criminal enforcement actions against Corporate Officers:

Five years imprisonment

$10,000 fine

Violations of IRS rulings may result in criminal enforcement action against Information Technology Managers:

Five years imprisonment

$10,000 fine

The Standard of Due Care for computer operations in a bank or other financial institution is usually higher than for other organizations. It may be necessary for your company to demonstrate a recovery plan was implemented *and exercises conducted.*

IRS Ruling 71-20 Revenue Ruling 71-20 1, 197 1-1 CB 392

Holds that taxpayer's records are required to be retained so long as the contents may become material in the adjudication of any internal revenue action.

International Standards Organization (ISO)

ISO 17799 is the major standard for information security. It is also a reliable guide for satisfying most mandated business continuity plan requirements.

American Institute of Certified Public Accountants (AICPA)

Statement of Auditing Standards SAS-70 & SAS-55

NIST National Institute of Standards and Technology

Review literature and laboratory publications regarding generally accepted principles and practices.

APPENDIX B

Regulations Chart

This chart of regulations and their scope of applicability are intended as a guide to help organizations decide how to achieve compliance. It is not all inclusive. It is not intended to substitute for legal and audit opinions and should not be construed to do so.

Legislative Requirements for Business Continuity and Disaster Recovery Planning		
Sector	Legislation	Requirements
Medical/ Hospitals	HIPAA Regulations	Regulations covering electronic security and transmission of patient records. A documented, tested disaster recovery plan is required.
Financial Services and Banking	FFIEC FIL-67-97	Board of directors is responsible for ensuring that comprehensive business resumption and contingency plans have been implemented to encompass distributed computing and external service bureaus.
	Comptroller of Currency BC-177 (1983, 1987) superceded by FFIEC and Federal Home Loan Bank Bulletin R-67 (1986) superceded by FFIEC	Requires banking institutions to develop and maintain business recovery plans.

Legislative Requirements for Business Continuity and Disaster Recovery Planning		
Sector	Legislation	Requirements
	Inter-Agency Policy from Federal Financial Institutions Examination Council (FFIEC-1989, revised and made stronger 1997)	Requires business wide resumption planning and extends regulation to require contingency plans from any service bureaus or outsourcing companies that service such banks.
Public Companies	SEC Regulations	Reasonable safeguards for information. Boards of directors and senior management are accountable.
	Foreign Corrupt Practices Act (1977)	Requires that publicly-held corporations provide reasonable protection for information systems and holds management accountable.
All Companies	IRS Procedure 86-19	Legal backup and recovery requirements for computer records containing tax data.
eCommerce Transactions	Consumer Credit Protection Act (CCPA) section 2001 Title IX (1992)	Due diligence for availability of data in electronic funds transfers, including point of sale.
Federal Government	Computer Security Act	Requires security plans for all federal computer systems to assure data integrity, availability, and confidentiality.
	FEMA FRPG 01-94	All department and agency heads must formally plan for continuity of essential operations.
State Governments	Various State Dept. of Administrative Services Policies, e.g., Texas, (1 TAC 210.13(b)), Oregon's Dept. of Information Resources (ORS 291.038)	Policies assigning responsibility for contingency planning within state agencies.

APPENDIX C

Glossary

This Glossary is a partial list of industry terms. It covers key terms used in emergency management and business recovery.

Activation The implementation of recovery procedures, activities, and plans in response to an emergency or disaster declaration.

Alternate Site An alternate operating location to be used by business functions when the primary facilities are inaccessible.

Assessment Some measure that allows an organization to ascertain the amount of loss suffered should an event occur. Often this is expressed in terms of loss per day. Usually reflected as a linear loss, rather than showing any increases that may occur over time.

Business Continuity The process of returning essential services to an acceptable level of operation after a disaster.

BCP Document The printed and published copy of the business continuity plan. It is used as a manual for training recovery team members and as a guidebook during an actual disaster.

Business Continuity Plan A set of arrangements and procedures decided in advance that enable an organization to respond to a disaster and resume its critical operations within a defined time frame.

Damage Assessment The post-incident appraisal or determination of actual effects on human, physical, economic, and natural resources.

Disaster Any event that disrupts an organization's ability to perform critical business activities.

Disaster Management Team The group of managers designated to manage emergency recovery operations. It includes the business continuity coordinator and all recovery team leaders.

Financial Impact An operating expense that directly affects the financial position of the organization.

First Call-down The notification of the team leaders.

Mobilization The activation of the entire recovery organization in response to an emergency or disaster declaration.

Off-site Storage Site A storage area away from the main organization for critical documents, equipment, and supplies.

Preparedness Activities, programs, and systems developed prior to a disaster that are used to support and enhance mitigation of, response to, and recovery from disasters.

Recovery The process of planning for and/or implementing restoration of less time sensitive business operations and processes after critical business functions have resumed.

Recovery Point Objective A recovery point objective is the point where a process can be started with full intent to be kept running in an acceptable mode at an acceptable pace. Different processes, different devices, and different industries require very different start-up procedures. The varying conditions that define a recovery point objective cannot be designated until the interruption has occurred.

Recovery Site The permanent command center where an organization's operations are recovered.

Recovery Strategy The recovery strategy is the selection of necessary actions and the sequence in which to take them. Risk assessment and business impact analysis provide the information necessary to valid and timely decisions.

Recovery Time Objective The recovery time objective is the period of time from a business interruption to the recovery of a service or process. The standard recovery time is seventy-two hours time or less. When an interruption has occurred, speed of response to restore becomes a critical factor in itself. Downtime is deterioration time. The longer a business operation is unable to function, the longer it takes to restart and get back up to speed. The time objective will be to restart critical functions as soon as possible to stop any resources drain.

Recovery Window A period of time in which time-sensitive business operations must be resumed.

Response The reaction to an incident or emergency in order to assess the level of containment and to control required activity.

Responsibility The state of being responsible, accountable, or answerable, as for a task or obligation.

Restoration The process of planning for and implementing full-scale business operations that allow the organization to return to a normal service level.

Risk A possible event that can cause disruption such as: natural disasters, human error, a crime, civil unrest, terrorism, or non-compliance.

Second Call-down The notification of the sub-team members.

Stabilization The point at which all recovery personnel have completed emergency tasks, and all stress and health-related issues have been resolved.

Sub-team Individuals responsible for specific functions under the team leader.

Tasks Specific activities assigned to individuals on each team to complete the team responsibilities.

Temporary Command Site A location where the contingency organization can gather to start recovery operations prior to establishing the permanent command site.

APPENDIX D

Sample Security Audits

Sample Physical Security Audit

1. Name of client company:
2. Interview with:
3. Title:
4. Date:
5. Address:
6. Facility name or location:
7. Main activity?

Human Resources

8. Total number of employees?
9. Number of full time:
10. What type?
11. Outsourced?
12. By whom?
13. Extent of investigation on background?
14. Number of part-time:
15. Screening used?
16. What type?
17. Background checks done?
18. What type?
19. Number of temps:
20. Agency used?
21. Screening used?
22. What type?
23. Background checks done?
24. What type?
25. Number of shifts:
26. Shift hours:
27. Shift rotation?
28. Outside maintenance crew?
29. Name?
30. Screening used?
31. What type?
32. Background checks done?
33. What type?
34. Have keys?
35. Alarm code?
36. How long?
37. How many? Total?
38. Number of full time?
39. Number of part-time?
40. Number of temps?
41. Hours? Days?
42. Do they remove trash?
43. Is trash checked before removal?
44. Is trash shredded before removal?
45. Who controls maintenance crews?
46. Who controls their entry and exit?
47. Union shop?
48. Employees allowed to leave building on breaks?
49. Do you inspect all employee packages entering and leaving the building?
50. Any contract employees?
51. What agency or company used?
52. Have keys?
53. Alarm codes?
54. Screening used?

55. What type?
56. Background checks done?
57. What type?
58. Who do they report to?

Security Clearances

59. Is government work done here?
60. Degree of classification?
61. How are documents stored?
62. What is security during manufacture?
63. What is classification of finished product?
64. Are government inspectors on premises?
65. Any threats experienced?
66. Locker room incidents?

Physical Threats

67. Is facility subject to natural disastrous phenomena?
68. Describe natural risks in detail.
69. Describe type of fence, walls, buildings, and physical perimeter barriers.
70. Is fencing of acceptable height, design, and construction?
71. Condition of fencing?
72. Is material stored near fencing?
73. Poles or trees near fencing?
74. Small buildings near fencing?
75. Undergrowth near fencing?
76. Is there an adequate clear zone on both sides along fencing?
77. Can vehicles drive up to fencing?
78. Wire mesh on windows?
79. Do storm sewers or utility tunnels breach the barrier?
80. Are they secured?
81. Is perimeter barrier regularly maintained and inspected?

Alarms

82. Facility alarm system?
83. Name of alarm company:
84. Address:
85. Phone Number:
86. UL approved?
87. Locally monitored?
88. Last tested?
89. Employees trained?
90. Number of employees with access codes?
91. No access restrictions:
92. With access restrictions:
93. Describe restrictions:
94. Do alarms warn of these situations or conditions:
95. Fire?
96. Smoke?
97. Panic?
98. Penetration?
99. Water flow?
100. Motion?
101. Heat?
102. Glass breakage?
103. Medical?
104. Sound?
105. Touch?
106. Proximity sensors?

Access Control-Personnel

107. How many exterior doors on premises?
108. Are they all alarmed?
109. Entry during working hours?
110. Exit during working hours?
111. Central station alarm?
112. Guards on site?
113. Key holder?
114. Overhead doors?
115. Number of doors and locations for employee usage.
116. CCTV used at exterior doors?
117. Monitored?
118. Taped?
119. Reviewed?
120. By whom?
121. How often?
122. How are they controlled?

123. Electric locks?
124. Pass card?
125. Tracking?
126. Access only?
127. Is CCTV used to observe exterior perimeter?
128. Monitored?
129. Taped?
130. Reviewed?
131. By whom?
132. How often?
133. Emergency door?
134. How is it controlled?
135. Any unprotected doors to exterior?
136. Roof?
137. Location of administrative offices?
138. Sensitive material stored inside?
139. How secured?
140. Back-up copies of sensitive materials made?
141. Locked?
142. Alarmed?
143. CCTV in use?
144. Monitored?
145. Taped?
146. Reviewed?
147. By whom?
148. How often?
149. Who has access?
150. Cleaning crews?
151. When are offices locked?
152. Who is responsible to check security at end of day?
153. How are records stored?
154. How are they secured?
155. Are vaults equipped with temperature thermostats (rate-of-rise, etc.)?
156. Offices equipped with sprinklers?
157. Fire extinguishers?
158. Smoke detectors?
159. Are cabinets and desks locked?
160. Are individual offices locked?
161. Designated computer rooms?
162. Type of fire protection?

Access Control–Receiving Materiel

163. How many shipping docks?
164. CCTV in use?
165. Monitored?
166. Taped?
167. Reviewed?
168. By whom?
169. How often?
170. Hours of operation?
171. Method of transportation?
172. Describe inventory control in warehouse.
173. Describe inventory control at docks.
174. What supervision is exercised at docks?
175. Describe security policy/procedures in warehouse.
176. In dock area.
177. How are truck drivers controlled?
178. Is there a waiting room for truck drivers?
179. Is it separated from company employees?
180. What is the method of accounting for material received and shipped?

Shipping

181. Is shipping done by parcel post?
182. What is the control at point of packaging?
183. Who transports packages to post office?
184. What is the method of transport?
185. Where is the pick-up point at the plant?
186. What controls are exercised over the transport vehicles?
187. Are inspections of operations made?
188. Who conducts them?
189. How often?
190. Reports made?

Employees and Visitors

191. How are visitors escorted through facility?

192. Badges worn?
193. Is trash stored outside of the building?
194. How is it secured from outsiders?
195. Is there adequate exterior protective lighting?
196. Interior lighting adequate?
197. Parking area?
198. Are employees allowed to park personal vehicles next to facility?
199. How close?
200. Employee vehicles allowed overnight in lot?
201. Non-employee vehicles allowed overnight in lot?
202. Employees allowed to bring non-employees into facility?
203. With permission?
204. With/without badges?
205. Are non-employees required to sign in and out?
206. Are all visitors required to sign in/out?
207. Identification requested?
208. Are those logs kept?
209. How long and where?

Locks

210. Is there a grand-master, master, and sub-master system?
211. Describe the system in use-.
212. Are locks used all made by the same manufacturer?
213. Security type locks? (e.g., Medico)
214. Is there a record of issuance of locks?
215. Who is charged with handling key control?
216. Is the system adequate?
217. Describe control measures in use.
218. When are locks changed?
219. Are investigations made when keys are lost?
220. Are locks changed if keys are lost?

Physical Control

221. Describe physical control at each entrance.
222. Time clocks used?
223. Elevators?
224. Employees restricted to certain work areas?
225. How is that controlled?
226. Are groups allowed to visit and observe operations?
227. How are they controlled?
228. Employee uniforms?
229. Are colors used to identify work location for employees?
230. Are parking lots fenced off from production areas?
231. Is vehicle identification used?
232. Have you ever had a professional facility security review done?
233. Is it possible for persons to enter the facility during shift changes?

Emergency Planning

234. Do you have contingency plans?
235. What contingencies do they cover?
236. When were they last updated?
237. Who is in charge of document control?
238. Where are plans stored?
239. Do you have a disaster recovery plan?
240. When was it done?
241. Last update?
242. Has it been tested?
243. Who is in charge of the plan?
244. Do you have a business continuity plan?
245. When was it done?
246. Last update?
247. Has it been tested in full?
248. Has it been tested in part?
249. Who is in charge of the plan?

Personnel Security

250. Is a package-pass control system used? Describe the system.
251. Are employee signatures available for comparison?

252. Are current photographs maintained of all employees?
253. Where are they stored?
254. What action is taken when an employee is caught stealing?
255. Are employees allowed to carry personal property/lunch boxes into work area?

Trash Control

256. Is trash periodically inspected?
257. By whom?
258. How often?

Adverse Incidents

259. Have you experienced a security problem in the last two years?
260. Number of problems?
261. Describe each problem.
262. How was it resolved?
263. Any theft occurrences?
264. Systematic or casual?
265. Patterns established?
266. Violence?
267. Describe theft history:
268. Theft or contamination of company information?
269. Describe:
270. Physical penetration into facility?
271. Describe:
272. Theft of personal property from inside facility?
273. Describe:
274. Damage or vandalism inside or outside of facility?
275. Theft from autos?
276. Theft of company property?
277. Theft of raw materials?
278. Theft of supplies?
279. Theft of parts or equipment?
280. Have you ever reported an incident to a law enforcement agency?
281. How many times in the last two years?
282. Local police?
283. County sheriff?
284. State police or regulating agency?
285. Federal law enforcement?
286. Military related agency?
287. Is it still a pending investigation?
288. What was the outcome?
289. Did it involve employees?
290. Past employees?
291. Current employees?
292. Contracted employees?
293. Temps?
294. Cleaning crew?
295. Non-company related outsider?
296. What was dollar loss?
297. Was property or information involved?
298. Did company sustain physical damage or vandalism?
299. Was stolen property recovered?
300. Where?
301. By whom?
302. Was the source of information detected?
303. Do you have a copy of offense report?
304. Was an arrest made?
305. Was the suspect prosecuted?
306. How many suspects were involved?
307. What was motive?
308. Was alarm system compromised?
309. How?
310. Was entry to facility forced?
311. Entry method?
312. Exit method?
313. Method used to transport stolen goods?
314. Do you have suspects?
315. Have they been interviewed?
316. Did you conduct the interview?
317. Have you ever used the services of a licensed private investigator?
318. Who?
319. How often?
320. When?

321. For what reason?
322. Did this matter subsequently involve civil litigation?
323. What was the outcome?
324. Would you use that investigator again? Explain.
325. Was property recovered?
326. Did this involve criminal proceedings?
327. Was the matter turned over to law enforcement authorities?
328. Is the matter still under investigation?
329. What was that outcome?
330. Is the matter currently in the court system?

Security Guidelines For Employees

331. Does your company have travel safety policy or guidelines for employees?
332. Do you check with any federal agencies before traveling abroad?
333. Does your travel agency provide risk alerts when booking travel abroad?
334. Has any stolen property ever turned up in, on, or adjacent to your property?
335. Do you allow your employees to work for other employers who may be competitors?
336. Do you allow your employees to work part-time jobs for other employers?
337. Do you have any restrictions?
338. Do you have a card access system installed?
339. Are all employees issued cards for access?
340. Are some cards restricted access?
341. Who controls the card access programs?
342. Are they supervised by a senior manager?
343. Are logs periodically reviewed for errors?
344. How soon after termination are employee's access rights removed from card access?
345. Who has that responsibility?
346. Describe the process.
347. How soon after termination are employee's access rights removed from computer access?
348. Who has that responsibility?
349. Describe the process.

Security Effectiveness

350. Do you believe your facility is secure and can withstand a physical penetration attempt from outside? Explain.
351. Do your employees feel safe in the workplace? Explain.
352. Do you believe your company can recover the essential business functions within a critical time frame after a disaster at an alternate location? Explain.
353. Do you believe your company can recovery essential IT functions within a critical time frame after a disaster? Explain.
354. Do you believe that your company polices adequately protect against civil litigation? Explain.
355. Do you believe your company information is safe from unauthorized access, covert use, and unauthorized distribution? Explain.

Sample Information Security Audit

Overall Security-Central Site

1. Has a formal disaster recovery plan been developed for your organization?
2. Tested?
3. Updated regularly?
4. Have disaster recovery teams been identified and trained?
5. Have operating procedures been established to maintain business if the computer center is not operational?
6. Have vital computer operations been identified and prioritized?
7. Is there a person designated as security officer?

8. Are premises always tended or patrolled?
9. Are doors to critical areas kept locked, even during work hours?
10. Are log-in procedures required for entry during work hours?
11. Have advertisements of the location of the central computer facility been eliminated from signs, maps, and directory listings of the organization?
12. Are tours by the public through the computer facility discouraged?
13. Is the location of the computer center kept out of the public eye, and have all directing signs been removed?
14. Is the computer center closed to the public?
15. Are visitors required to be signed in and out by authorized personnel?
16. Do receptionists notify spaces to be visited upon clearance of visitors?
17. Does console operator always face visitors?
18. Are escorts required to accompany visitors to critical areas?
19. Are all personnel sufficiently security conscious to challenge any employees without badges, or any unidentified visitors?
20. Is the building's construction, including walls, roof, and floors, made of noncombustible materials to reduce the chance of fire?
21. Are the walls near critical equipment or media constructed of materials that cannot be easily penetrated?
22. Do the walls extend from the building's structural floor to the building's structural ceiling and not from raised floors to lowered ceilings?
23. Is the computer facility physically separate from other departments?
24. In multi-story buildings, is the computer facility located on an upper floor to reduce the risk of external penetration and flood damage?
25. Are the computer rooms and tape/disk storage library separated by noncombustible walls with a minimum fire resistance fire rating of two hours?
26. Have viewing windows into the central computer facility been eliminated?
27. Does the tape/disk storage vault have a door that will automatically close in case of fire, and does it have proper alarms and automatic fire-retardant dispensing equipment?
28. Are ceilings watertight to prevent leaks from floors above?
29. Are floor lifter tools mounted near portable fire extinguishers and duly marked?
30. Are automatic fire dampers installed in the air conditioning ducts and fresh-air ducts supplying the computer room?
31. In case of a fire, will the dampers cut off airflow that would feed the flames?
32. Are paper and other combustible supplies, with the exception of those needed for immediate use, stored outside the computer room?
33. Has an un-interruptible power supply (UPS) and/or a backup generator been installed? These systems may offer temporary protection that allows an orderly shutdown should the normal power supply fail, or they may offer a long-term electrical backup. These systems should be tested at least quarterly.
34. Does the computer center, especially the CPU, have its own separate incoming power supply and power cables?
35. Are emergency power shutdown controls installed at all fire exits?
36. Are circuit breaker panels properly marked as to the equipment being serviced to permit ready and expeditious reference?
37. Are batter-powered emergency lights provided throughout the facility?
38. Are the following housekeeping policies in effect:

    Prohibit eating and drinking in the computer room?

    Prohibit smoking in the computer room?

Clean equipment covers and work surfaces daily?

Clean floors regularly?

Is space under raised floors cleaned regularly?

Dump waste baskets and other trash containers outside of the computer room to avoid excess dust?

Unpack equipment and paper supplies outside the equipment room to reduce dust?

39. Enforce the entry and exit policies for all personnel?
40. Are programmers generally not allowed in the computer room? For proper segregation of duties, programmers should be prohibited from entering the computer room except in an emergency.
41. Is there a prohibition to keep employees working on highly sensitive data from performing all their own operations (delivery of data, tape handling, computer operations, tape storage and release, receiving custody of results)?
42. Are employees prohibited from working where sensitive data or programs are stored?
43. Within the past six months, have the lock-and-key control procedures been reviewed as they affect sensitive areas?
44. Are there systematic procedures for the handling and disposal of sensitive materials?
45. Does the room layout allow supervisors to watch the progress of classified jobs at all times?
46. Are systems programmers present whenever manufacturer's diagnostics are run?
47. Are combinations to safes, locks, and padlocks changed at least once a year and whenever key personnel leave?
48. Upon termination of an employee, is a checklist used to assure the following materials are obtained from the employee before the final check is issued:
    A. Keys and ID badges?
    B. All hand-receipted or sensitive documentation or data?
    C. All operators' procedures?
    D. All program documentation?
    E. All library books and other borrowed materials?
    F. All organization-issued equipment and tools?
    G. Any documentation on incomplete tasks?
49. If it is an old facility with outside windows, has the glass been replaced by reinforced panes or otherwise protected by external screens?
50. Are special precautions taken if employees or others are on strike or picketing?
51. Are lists of emergency phone number prepared, maintained, and posted?
52. Are names and phone numbers of key personnel to be called in case of emergencies clearly posted in all critical areas?
53. Are these lists changed when a person moves, is promoted, or quits?
54. Are phones showing emergency numbers readily available in all critical areas?
55. In the case of power outages, have provisions been made to seek emergency assistance even though power and telephone service have been disrupted?
56. Are emergency lights aimed at all workstations that handle classified jobs?
57. If the facility does not operate around the clock, are fire, water, and intrusion alarms connected to permanently manned guard stations?
58. Have emergency procedures been developed for bomb threats, fire, wind, and flooding?
59. Are emergency procedures clearly posted?
60. Do telephone operators and receptionists have a standard procedure to follow in event of a bomb threat or other emergency?

61. If the computer center is vulnerable to riot or vandalism, has contact been established with a local law enforcement agency, and is there a contingency plan to supply help to the center promptly in the event trouble occurs?
62. Are there automatic alarm systems for:
    A. Fire?
    B. Temperature control?
    C. Humidity control?
    D. Voltage fluctuations?
    E. Chilled water temperature?
    F. Access control?
    G. Air conditioning compressor overheats?
    H. Coolant flow?
    I. Motor generator overheats?
63. Do posts carrying fire alarms or fire extinguishers have stripes or signs encircling them so it is easy to identify location of fire equipment from any viewpoint?
64. If a Halon or similar fire suppression system is installed with central containers and a master control, are procedures in place and are people properly trained to assure protection of individuals before the fire suppression system is energized?
65. Are fire alarms conveniently located and prominently marked in all critical areas?
66. Are hand-held extinguishers available within fifty feet of all electrical equipment?
67. Is there an automatic sprinkler system?
68. Has the tape and disk library vault been certified as having a four-hour fire rating?
69. Was the library vault designed to keep its contents safe from steam and water damage in addition to heat and flame?
70. If there is a possibility of water damage from a fire on floors above the computer installation? Are there covers for machines and is there adequate drainage?
71. Is the computer site carefully chosen to be as safe as possible from natural and other disasters?
72. If the institution is in a location subject to flooding, have steps been taken to place the data processing installation and programmer offices and files above the high water level?
73. Are there drains in the floors of critical areas?
74. Are regular safety inspections held to avoid accumulation of inflammables, blocked aisles, or inadvertent safety violations due to equipment rearrangement?
75. Have potential salvage and recovery operations been discussed and outlined?
76. Will backup systems have adequate resources available to allow emergency work to be run?
77. Has the physical protection at each remote terminal location been reviewed and evaluated even though these locations may not be under direct main office supervision?
78. If using a password system, are the passwords "masked" as they are input?
79. Are passwords changed at regular intervals?
80. If stand-alone minicomputers are distributed throughout the organization:

    Are the programs, data files, and operating software backed up and stored off-premises?

    Are there alternate systems for processing this work?

    Have they been included in your disaster recovery plan?

    Are scaled-down library procedures and controls established to govern the handling and storage of critical files at remote sites?
81. Is password protection used throughout the system?
82. Is an authorization function used that relates password, location, operator ID, time of day, security level of termi-

nal, and security level of the communication patch before access is allowed?

83. Are passwords used to protect sensitive files against unauthorized entry?
84. Are all users sufficiently sensitive to the need for security of passwords?
85. Are passwords encrypted?
86. Has the authorization algorithm been tested by trying:
    A. To gain access to a safeguarded program or file while not authorized to do so?
    B. To use a legitimate name and an illegitimate password in an attempt to access a legitimate program or file?
    C. To use a legitimate name and password to legitimately gain access to a file and perform an unauthorized operation?
    D. To violate file access limitation where you have legitimate access, i.e., try to delete a record where you only have access to read?
    E. To access the system from a remote location outside of regular business hours using a legitimate name, password, and location?
    F. To use an obsolete password the day after it was changed?
    G. To log on with a legitimate name and password from an unusual location?
    H. To log on and then let terminal activities go dormant for an extended period to see if the terminal is automatically logged off?
    I. To test the limit of log on attempts by repeatedly entering illegitimate names, passwords, etc.?
87. Is it impossible to change the security tables from any terminal other than the master security terminal and/or with the systems administrator's password?
88. Are programmers prohibited from changing the security tables?
89. Is the operator's console prohibited from changing the security tables?
90. Is there a trouble log, and is diagnosis continued on each problem until the person, software component, or device that has malfunctioned can be isolated?
91. Are there sufficient controls in the shop so that the number of times a job is initiated is logged and compared against the master schedule? Note: A simple way to obtain a second copy of output is to schedule a job twice and let it run twice producing two sets of output.
92. Is it possible for the console operator to reset the computer's internal time-of-day clock?
93. Does violation of the security protection cause the job to be instantly aborted and a message written on the master security terminal and on the security log?
94. Is the sign-off procedure for a remote terminal as elaborate as the sign-on procedure?

    Note: *Where critical information is involved, an airtight sign-off procedure can assure that a perpetrator does not tap a line and take over access with full privileges merely by canceling the legitimate user's sign-off message.*
95. Are the lead technical personnel believed to be trustworthy?
96. Has a background investigation been performed on each of them?
97. Are they bonded or otherwise insured?

Software and Programs

98. If there is an arrangement for off-site computer backup, have you tested it to be sure it will work?
99. Have standards been established to provide for audit trails, program approvals, and appropriate activity logs for any program dealing with sensitive data?

100. Have the programming standards for sensitive programs been reviewed with security officials and the internal auditors?
101. Are all errors and corrections made by new employees double checked?
102. Are totals and record counts programmed into routines that manipulate sensitive files so that a file once established can be monitored without a transaction-by-transaction audit of every production run?
103. Are the number of transactions to be processed as input compared with the number actually processed?
104. Are out-of-range values automatically flagged?
105. Is the computer charge-out system protected against improper or erroneous charges?
106. Are employees with access to the system prohibited from having their own accounts or records within the system?
107. To avoid conflict, are employees prohibited from being members of populations affected by the programs they write, i.e., if I am a payroll programmer, is my paycheck either written manually or by a payroll system I have not written?
108. If a classified job reaches an abnormal end, is the shift supervisor immediately notified to oversee the restart or termination of the job, and is a report prepared describing the abnormal end and the procedures followed to restart the job?
109. For the computer programs identified as sensitive, have the following been safeguarded:
    A. The source program?
    B. The source listing?
    C. The program documentation?
    D. The object code (machine-language version of the program)?
110. Are active tapes and disks retained in the library?
111. Are important history tapes and disks retained in the archives?
112. Is someone assigned to review the system logs on a daily basis to look for illegal file accesses and other security violations?
113. Are label overrides on a security log?
114. Are passwords and entries in authorization tables removed for each terminated employee?
115. Are there protections against magnetic effects?
116. Do the disks have labels, and are these labels checked upon mounting?
117. Are there procedures for:

    Overwriting and cleaning of disks?

    Retiring disks from service?

    Does the operating system issue tape mount messages and check the labels of the tapes that are mounted?

    Are the labels of the tapes that are mounted checked?

    Are all scratch tapes and work tapes properly accounted for at the end of the each processing run and each production shift?
118. Does the library procedures manual cover:
    A. Initial receipt and logging of new tapes?
    B. Labeling of new tapes?
    C. Assigning tapes from the available pool?
    D. Pulling tapes for a production run and the keeping of appropriate logs?
    E. Returning tapes from a run and the completion of those logs?
    F. Procedures to assure that a tape cannot be borrowed, copied, and returned without discovery?
    G. Overwriting of released tapes containing proprietary information?
    H. Overwriting followed by cleaning of tapes?

I. Retiring tapes from service?

J. Sending tapes to the archives?

K. Recalling tapes from the archives?

L. Receiving tapes from a remote location?

M. Assigning test tapes to a programmer?

119. Steam is an additional hazard to magnetic tapes. Have the safes and vaults been certified against this hazard?

120. Are stored tapes protected against magnetic fields that are strong enough to affect the recorded data?

121. Are tapes withdrawn from the library required to be logged out?

122. If so, are they signed for and duly receipted on return?

123. Is there a systematic follow-up procedure for tapes that are overdue?

APPENDIX E

Business Impact Analysis Forms

SECTION 1:
Business Impact Analysis

Date: ______________________________

Division: ______________________________

Business Unit: ______________________________

Contact Name: ______________________________

Contact Phone: ______________________________

Contact E-mail: ______________________________

PART I:
Overview Of The Business Unit

1. Describe the general functions of the business unit:
2. Briefly describe the business unit's processes.
3. Which description best fits the unit?
   - ❑ Production/design/engineering/manufacturing unit or service.
   - ❑ Unit with direct client contact.
   - ❑ Unit that directly provides production/engineering/service support.
   - ❑ Unit responsible for marketing/sales/advertising.
   - ❑ Provides order taking or order entry.
   - ❑ Administrative.
   - ❑ Other:

4. Work day ranges from what time of day?
5. How many shifts do you operate per day? What are the shift times?
6. What is the average daily dollar volume processed by the unit?

   In revenue?

   In transactional dollars?
7. Does the unit have any peak volume or otherwise critical times? If the unit does, please list the times as well as the average dollar and item or transaction volumes processed at those times (indicate time of day, time of week, time of month, and time of year of peak volumes).

Part 2: *Work Flow Interdependencies*

This section is intended to document the flow of work to and from your unit. It also is intended to determine *how* the work gets to your unit and *how* your unit sends it out once it has been completed.

Work Received

1. Describe how the business unit receives information flow to enable it to generate services such as: list business units, in-house central computer systems, data processing service bureaus, or other organizations from which your unit receives work.
2. Of the total amount of incoming work your unit receives, what percentage comes through the following routes? (Must add up to 100 percent.)
   - ❑ E-mail
   - ❑ U.S. mail
   - ❑ Telephone or fax
   - ❑ Interoffice mail
   - ❑ Courier
   - ❑ Online information from the central computer systems
   - ❑ Reports or fiche copies generated from the central computer systems
   - ❑ Online information from external data processing services
   - ❑ Reports or fiche copies generated by external data processing services

Work Sent

3. Describe how the business unit sends information flow to enable it to generate services such as: list the units, in-house central computer systems, data processing service bureaus, or other organizations to which your unit sends completed work or information.
4. Of the total amount of outgoing work your unit produces, what percentage is sent through the following routes? (Must add up to 100 percent.)
   - ❑ E-mail
   - ❑ U.S. mail
   - ❑ Telephone or fax
   - ❑ Interoffice mail
   - ❑ Courier
   - ❑ Online information from the central computer systems
   - ❑ Reports or fiche copies generated from the central computer systems
   - ❑ Online information from external data processing services
   - ❑ Reports or fiche copies generated by external data processing services

Part 3:
LAN or PC Computer Resources

1. Which computer equipment does your unit use?
   - ❑ Stand-alone PCs
   - ❑ Stand-alone computers
   - ❑ Computers connected to a local area network (LAN)
2. How are the computers or LAN used?
   - ❑ General administrative or office functions (e.g., e-mail)
   - ❑ Gateway to the organization's mainframe computer systems and system applications
   - ❑ Other
3. Are the automation features of the computers or the LAN used by the unit critical to the timing and efficiency of the services the unit provides? Please describe.
4. Do those computers or the LAN directly support or provide information required to control your unit's operations? Please describe.

5. If the LAN or computers were unavailable for one business day, would there be a data entry or transaction backlog?

   ❑ Yes ❑ No (If no, skip next two questions.)

6. Estimate the amount of backlog in number of entries or transactions
   - On a normal business day
   - At the unit's most critical peak time
7. Estimate the hours it would take your current staff to eliminate the backlog. Please include the average hourly pay rate plus fringes for the staff.
   - Hours at current staffing on a normal business day.
   - Hours at current staffing at your unit's most critical peak time
   - Average pay rate per hour plus fringes for current staff

Part 4:
In-house Computer-based Information Systems

(Use as many sheets as necessary to cover all computer-based systems you utilize in your area.)

System or application (Specify): ______________________________

____

1. Would an outage of this system or application affect other revenue activities (e.g., investments, interest on funds, cash management) or balancing?
2. Does the system or application allow clients to access the system directly via the Internet?

   ❑ Yes ❑ No

3. If the system or application were unavailable to your unit for one business day, would there be a data entry or transaction backlog?

   ❑ Yes ❑ No

   If you answered yes, estimate the amount of backlog in number of entries or transactions:
   - On a normal business day.
   - At the unit's most critical peak time.

   Estimate the time it would take your current staff to eliminate the backlog. Please include the average hourly pay rate plus fringes for the staff.

- Hours at current staffing on a normal business day.
- Hours at current staffing at your unit's most critical peak time.
- Average pay rate per hour plus fringes for current staff.

4. Would a one-day delay in processing this system or application result in any regulatory fines or penalties due to missed deadlines or other reasons?

   ❑ Yes ❑ No

   If you answered yes, describe the reason for the penalty, the issuer of the penalty, and an average for such penalties.

5. After a disaster, within which time frame, recovery time objective (RTO), do you need to have access to this function for the above system/application? To what point, recovery point objective (RPO), must recovery be essential for the selected recovery window?

   ❑ Less than 1 hour
   ❑ 1–4 hours
   ❑ 4–8 hours
   ❑ 8–24 hours
   ❑ 2 days—1 week
   ❑ Other______________________________

6. Are there any peak periods associated with this system or application? Check those times that apply and include a brief explanation of the reason for the peak time for each.

   ❑ Daily
   ❑ Weekly
   ❑ Quarterly
   ❑ Monthly
   ❑ Month end
   ❑ Quarter end
   ❑ Year end
   ❑ Other (please specify)______________________________

Part 5:
Outsourced Data Processing

If the organization uses an external provider of information services, an assessment of the impact of the loss of applications must be made. Please answer the following questions. (The questions provided in the in-house computer systems questionnaire can also be used for outside services.)

1. Does the service provider have a disaster recovery plan and a business continuity plan?
2. Has the plan been tested?
3. When was the plan last tested, what were the test objectives, and what was the result of the test?
4. What percentage of total applications were tested?
5. What is the recovery time frame for the service provider's systems?
6. Do they consider your organization a high priority?
7. Was the network connecting your organization and the service provider tested?
8. Is there a network recovery plan for the service provider?
9. Where in the network recovery priorities is your organization?
10. If their system is accessed through the Internet, is their system backed up if their service is down?

Part 6: Regulatory And Legal Issues

Regulatory Issues

1. Are there any reporting requirements or deadlines that would be affected by a delay in or loss of the services your unit provides?
2. Would a delay in or loss of service result in any regulatory fines or penalties?
    a. List the regulations.
    b. Describe the conflict.
    c. Describe possible consequences (e.g., penalties).

Legal Issues

1. Will a delay in or loss of the services your unit provides result in possible legal liability, damages, or other public harm?
    a. List the legal issue.
    b. Describe the conflict.
    c. Describe possible consequences.

PART 7:
Transaction Volume Loss— Normal Business Day

Consider that your unit is unable to perform its functions as a result of a disaster on a normal business day. By how much would the transaction volume decrease? If the disaster extended through each period of time listed below, how much transaction volume might the company lose during each period? Fill in the appropriate dollar range (e.g., $0-50,000; $50,000-100,000) for each time period listed below.

What would the loss over time be if your business unit was down?

First half hour: - $__________________
Hour 1: - $__________________
Hour 2: - $__________________
Hour 3: - $__________________
Hours 4-12: - $__________________
Hours 13-24: - $__________________
Day 2: - $__________________
Days 3-7: - $__________________
Days 8-14: - $__________________
Days 15-29: - $__________________
Day 30 and beyond: - $__________________

PART 8:
Transaction Volume Loss— Peak Business Day

Consider that your unit is unable to perform its functions as a result of a disaster on a peak business day. By how much would the transaction volume decrease? If the disaster extended through each period of time listed below, how much transaction volume might the company lose during each period? Fill in the appropriate dollar range (e.g., $0-100,000; $100,000-500,000) for each time period listed below.

What would the loss over time be based on the following?

First half hour: - $__________________
Hour 1: - $__________________
Hour 2: - $__________________
Hour 3: - $__________________
Hours 4-12: - $__________________

Hours 13-24: - $________________
Day 2: - $________________
Days 3-7: - $________________
Days 8-14: - $________________
Days 15-29: - $________________
Day 30 and beyond: - $________________

Part 9:
Revenue Loss

1. Is this business function directly involved in activities that generate revenue? If so, describe. What systems or applications are utilized in the revenue generation activities?
2. Is this business function directly involved in billing or collection activities? If so, describe. What systems or applications are utilized in the billing or collection activities?
3. Would inability to conduct this business function affect business operations so as to interfere with the provision of services to customers? If so, how?
4. Would inability to conduct this business function cause customers to seek services or products from competitors? If so, please assess this impact.
5. Would inability to conduct this business function cause other, indirect impacts on revenue activities (e.g., interest lost on funds, investments)?
6. Summarize other revenue losses associated with impacts related to the inability to conduct this business function.

Part 10:
Additional Expenses

1. What are the types of additional expenses your organization would incur with the delay or loss of processing of this application, (e.g., productivity rates, lost revenue opportunities)?
2. Estimate the minimum length of time the support of this application could be denied your organization without incurring additional expense (e.g., overtime, extra services).

3. Would a delay in the availability of this application result in additional expenditures other than for labor or services (e.g., interest expense on bank loans, capital outlays)?
4. Estimate the amount of business backlog (e.g., number of orders, order entries, inquiries) incurred if this application were unavailable.
5. Would a delay in processing this application result in any regulatory fines or penalties for failure to provide services or to adhere to deadlines or government regulations? If so, describe.
6. Would a delay in processing the application result in legal liability, personal damage, or other public harm? If so, please describe.
7. Please describe any other impacts related to the delay or loss of this application that could result in additional expense to your organization on the reverse side of this page.

Part 11:
Embarrassment Or Confidence Loss

1. In your estimation, what are the most serious sources of embarrassment to your organization in regard to the delay in or complete loss of ability to process this application or provide this service, (e.g., damage to brand, communications with customers, promises missed)?
2. What is the potential liability of exposure to these problems and impact on the general public in terms of embarrassment to the organization?
3. What are the potential impacts, in terms of loss of public confidence and other measures, from the loss of capability to process this application or provide this service, (e.g., public trust)?

Part 12:
Client Loss

1. Would a delay in the processing of this application or provision of services cause clients to seek competitor services?
2. If yes, what percentage of corporate income do these clients represent?

3. How long do you think the client would tolerate an interruption of company services?
4. Would these clients return when services are resumed? If yes, would there be additional expenses associated with re-establishing the relationship? Please describe.

Section II:
Sample Business Unit's External Dependencies

Date: ______________________________

Division: ______________________________

Business Unit: ______________________________

Business Unit Contact Name: ______________________________

Contact Phone: ______________________________

Contact E-mail: ______________________________

1. Provide a list of all of your vendors and their complete contact information, and the equipment and/or supplies you purchase from them.
2. Do you have a centralized purchasing department? Do you also do your own department's purchasing?
3. Provide a list of your customers and rank-order them in terms of their current and expected purchase amounts. Also, information on all contractual obligations, including service level agreements.
4. Provide a list of private and public organizations or firms upon whom you depend for services, such as on-going consulting activities, software development, documentation (ISO 9000, for example), and other outsourced services.
5. Provide a list of organizations you are required to provide periodic reports. Specify the periodicity (daily/weekly/monthly/quarterly/annual) for these reports.

SECTION III:
Sample Business Unit's Vital Records Needs

Date: ______________________________

Division: ______________________________

Business Unit: ______________________________

Business Unit Contact Name: ______________________________

Contact Phone: ______________________________

Contact E-mail: ______________________________

Provide a list of **company policy manuals**, standard operating procedures, and other documents for your business unit in the following categories:

(Responsible Individual Assigned: ______________________________)

Should Always be Available	Critical Records Recoverable	Recoverable from Source

Provide a list of **paper records** for your business unit in the following categories:

(Responsible Individual Assigned: ______________________________)

Should Always be Available	Critical Records Recoverable	Recoverable from Source

Provide a list of **electronic records** for your business unit in the following categories:

(Responsible Individual Assigned: ______________________________)

Should Always be Available	Critical Records Recoverable	Recoverable from Source

Provide a list of **multimedia records** for your business unit in the following categories: (Include photographs, film, video, recordings, etc. that apply)

(Responsible Individual Assigned: ______________________________)

Should Always be Available	Critical Records Recoverable	Recoverable from Source

APPENDIX F

Sample Recovery Site Selection Checklist

Use the following checklist to assist in the identification of a suitable alternate site.[4]

Building

Questions	Answers
What is the square footage of the available space?	
Price per square foot?	
Do you have access to the whole floor?	
Other tenants on the floor?	
Is the space already built or is it completely empty?	
Do you have a floor plan of the space? If not, can you get one?	
How many floors are available?	
Is there space available in the basement or in an area without windows?	
Are the floors located above each other?	
What are the terms of the lease?	
Is a copy of the lease available?	
Is there access to the roof?	
Are there any problems core drilling between floors?	

Questions	Answers
What are the characteristics of the ceiling in the office space? (Hard lit, removable panels, etc.)	
How old is the building?	
Has the building ever been renovated? If so, when and how?	
Are there any union restrictions in the building?	
When is the space available?	

4. The checklist has been created by various unknown facilities experts.

Parking

Questions	Answers
Does the building have outside parking available? If so how many spaces?	
Does the building have a multi-floor parking structure? If so, is it attached to the building?	
Does the parking lot have lights?	
How many entrances are there into the parking structure?	
Are these entrances secured? If so, how?	
Are the parking spaces reserved? If not, can they be?	

Security

Questions	Answers
Is the entrance to the property secured?	
Is it secured with gates around the perimeter?	
Is there security card access into the building?	
Is there security card access on the elevator?	
Is there a security desk in the main lobby of the building?	

Questions	Answers
Is the security desk manned 24 x 7?	
How many security personnel are on staff after normal business hours?	
Do the security guards walk the property? If so, how often? How long does the walk-thru take?	
Are there any times when the security desk is not staffed?	
Are there security cameras that monitor the entrances? Elevators? Parking structures? Roof access? Stair wells? Lobby areas? Hallways?	
What security firm are you using?	

Telecommunications

Questions	Answers
Is the building connected to any of the telecommunications SONET Fiber Ring?	
What telecommunication carriers are providing service into this building already?	
Does this building have its own telecommunications company that offers voice/data and Internet services to the tenants?	
Are there multiple entrances into the building for telecommunication services? If so, from what direction are the conduits coming?	
Can satellite antennas be installed on the roof? If so, is there an additional charge?	
Are there any problems or restrictions installing communications cabling in the riser of the building? Can you physically see the riser rooms for telecommunication cabling?	

Questions	Answers
Is the riser room for telecommunications cabling located in the same room as electrical panels or janitor closets?	
Are the telecommunication rooms on each floor shared with other tenants?	

Power

Questions	Answers
Is there a generator in the building to provide power backup in the event of power failures? If so, is this available to tenants?	
Can a backup generator be installed on the property, if needed?	
How much power is available on each floor?	
How much power is available to you?	
Can additional power be added if required?	
Do you have a blueprint of the power distribution?	
Have the electrical cables ever been replaced? If so, when?	
How often do the tenants experience electrical outages in this building?	

Cabling Infrastructure

Questions	Answers
How many riser cable pairs are available from the building MPOP (Main Point of Presence) to the open floors for telecommunication services?	
Are there any fiber cables installed between the MPOP room to the floors that are AV?	

Questions	Answers
Are there voice and data cables already installed to office locations? If so, what are the characteristics of the cables? Can you get a copy of the cabling infrastructure documentation?	
Does the voice and data cable need to be installed in conduit? Does the cable need to be plenum (fireproof)?	

Air Conditioning

Questions	Answers
Is the space provided with air conditioning?	
What are the hours of operation for the air conditioning?	
Can you install your own air conditioning system in locations where you need them? If so, are there any restrictions?	
How is air conditioning provided in and throughout the building?	

Deliveries

Questions	Answers
Is there a loading dock available in the building? If so, describe.	
What are the hours of operation for the loading dock?	
Is the loading dock secured with a guard?	
Is the loading dock monitored by security cameras?	
How many freight elevators are there?	
Are the freight elevators self-operated or does a designated elevator operator control them?	
What is the size of the freight elevators?	

Questions	Answers
Can the freight elevators be reserved? If so, are there any restrictions?	

Fire, Life, and Safety

Questions	Answers
Is this building provided with a fire, life, and safety system? If so, describe.	
Has there ever been a fire in this building? If so, explain.	

Data Center Room

Questions	Answers
Is there an existing data center room in the available space?	
Is there a raised floor in the data center room?	
Is there a power distribution system installed in this room?	
Do you have the schematics for the power distribution system?	
Is there an Uninterrupted Power Supply (UPS) system installed in the room? If so, can you have the specifications on it? If so, how old is it? If so, are the batteries gel filled?	
Is this room environmentally controlled separate from the building system?	
What is the square footage and dimension of the room?	

APPENDIX G

Sample Team Templates

Disaster Management Team

Upon notification of a disaster, the disaster management team determines the extent of the damage. The recovery management team reviews the disaster's impact on various operations within the department and the feasibility of performing normal business operations at the main facility. It is up to the disaster management team to monitor all aspects of the recovery process and to receive reports from each team leader confirming recovery. Information collected during the recovery process is used for post-recovery evaluation and training.

Name	Responsibility	Contact Information
<Names>	Business Continuity Coordinator	Phones: work, home, cell, pager
	Crisis Management Team Leader	
	Call Response Team Leader	
	Logistics Support Team Leader	
	IT/IS Team Leader	
	Business Units Team Leader	

Business Continuity Coordinator Responsibilities

The business continuity coordinator has the ultimate responsibility to declare a disaster, activate the plan, and begin recovery. The business continuity coordinator receives first notification of a disaster and activates the recovery process. Within one hour, the business continuity coordinator notifies executive management. Once notified, the business continuity coordinator performs the tasks on the company recovery checklist. During a disaster, the duties of the business continuity coordinator include the following:

- Initiate business continuity proceedings and disaster declarations
- Coordinate management decisions and make final decisions
- Coordinate recovery activities
- Ensure the safety and well-being of on-site employees
- Document and monitor the recovery process; establish methods for evaluating the business continuity plan
- Monitor and control all disaster-related expenses

Call Center Team

The call center team is charged with receiving and processing calls from internal and external contacts.

Contact Information

Name	Responsibility	Contact Information
	Team Leader	W: H: C: P:
	Team Member	W: H: C: P:
	Team Member	W: H: C: P:

Call Center Team Responsibilities

- Answer and respond to incoming phone inquires
- Team leader to contact team
- Remind team to bring cell phones and chargers
- Team leader to report head count to HR
- Direct team to report to off-site location as directed by management

Call Center Team Tasks

Incoming Calls

- Answer inbound calls and direct to appropriate personnel
- Take and distribute messages to appropriate personnel

Outbound Calls/contacts

- Contact customers with current jobs within seventy-two hours
- Contact other customers as need arises or on a need-to-know basis
- Return messages from inbound call center
- Schedule and conduct face-to-face customer visits if deemed necessary

Equipment/Supplies Required

- Phone system
- Desk/table/chairs
- Office supplies—pens, paper, etc.
- Computer, modem, printer

Important Documents and Location

- Call-down worksheet and employee checklist located at recovery site entry desk

Crisis Management Team

The crisis management recovery team function, on a daily basis, is to be prepared to manage the dissemination of information, provide for continuation of payroll, deal with individuals with special needs resulting from the crisis, respond to legal issues related to the crisis, and maintain the safety and security of organization property and personnel.

Contact Information

Name	Responsibility	Contact Information
	Team Leader	W: H: C: P:
	Team Member	W: H: C: P:
	Team Member	W: H: C: P:

Crisis Management Team Responsibilities

- Account for all employees
- Determine casualties/physical and mental welfare
- Determine the welfare of non-hospitalized employees
- Notify employees when they can return to work and where they will be located
- Provide benefit assistance to employees and employees' families
- Coordinate counseling services for employees and employees' families
- Determine if legal counsel needs to be contacted
- Develop company's public response to disaster
- Secure disaster site and recovery site
- Assure all employees receive their pay on schedule
- Communicate to employees when to return to work
- Review any contracts or legal questions that may arise.

Crisis Management Team Tasks

- Conduct head count (see appendix for list)
- Determine if anyone is injured
- Contact family members of injured
- Designate employee communication methods (hotline, bulletin board, etc.) for two-way communication
- Communicate with employees for the status/condition of injured employees
- Communicate to employees when they can return to work and where
- Coordinate resources for employee needs (counselors, etc.)
- Coordinate placement of employees to monitor disaster site and recovery site for safety and security of equipment and documents from looting
- Communicate official public response to the disaster to customer service for inbound calls and sales for outbound client calls

Equipment/Supplies Required

- HR/payroll system
- Desk/chairs
- Office supplies—pens, paper, etc.
- Computer, modem, printer
- Checklist of employees and emergency contact names and numbers
- Cell phones

Important Documents and Location

- Employee listings/emergency contacts in file cabinet #1, third floor
- Checklist listing the following: employee name, ok, deceased, injured, hospital, condition, emergency contact; off-site storage–Box XYZ
- Local resources of counselors, pastors; yellow pages.
- Payroll provider information–phone numbers, contacts, etc., in file cabinet #2, third floor.

Sub-team: Safety and Security

The safety and security sub-team is charged with providing and maintaining safety and security of the property at the recovery site and the disaster site along with the safety of all associates.

Contact Information

Name	Responsibility	Contact Information
	Team Leader	W: H: C: P:
	Team Member	W: H: C: P:
	Team Member	W: H: C: P:

Team Responsibilities

- Provide security for damaged site
- Secure the new work location
- Provide a safe work environment at the new work location
- Monitor the people working on the recovery process
- Maintain contact with public officials–fire department, police department, city officials to let them know what is going on

Team Tasks

- Provide a means of identifying company employees along with public officials to enter the new temporary location
- Coordinate information with the public information leader so information can be given to public officials
- Establish security perimeter at the corners of the building so only authorized people are able to enter the damaged sites
- Arrange for transportation of team members to and from their duty assignments

Equipment/Supplies Required

- Two to three phones
- Listing of employee phone numbers
- Flashlights and flood lights
- Emergency phone numbers
- Walkie-talkies (two-way radios)
- Hard hats, gloves, and other personal protective equipment

Important Documents and Location

- Risk management files; H:\BCP\riskmgmt
- Database of employee information; H:\Personnel\employees

Sub-team: Public Information

The public information sub-team is charged with maintaining a flow of relevant information to media, authorities, and stakeholders.

Contact Information

Name	Responsibility	Contact Information
	Team Leader	W: H: C: P:
	Team Member	W: H: C: P:
	Team Member	W: H: C: P:

Team Responsibilities

- Responsible for collecting accurate and timely information regarding disaster team areas
- Provide information and status/updates to media, authorities, and stakeholders
- Advise BCC of status/progress of all communications
- Provide media access to appropriate spokesperson(s)

Team Tasks

- Collect accurate and timely information regarding disaster team areas
- Email/fax news releases to media, authorities, stakeholder lists
- Arrange news conferences
- Update periodically BCC and media contacts on information releases
- Provide guide/spokesperson for on-site media
- Ensure 24/7 availability of spokesperson(s)

Equipment/Supplies Required

- PC or laptop, printer, phone, fax machine

- Table and chairs
- Wireless Palm Pilot capable of sending and receiving email (in case of power outage)
- Quiet, secure location for audio media

Important Documents and Location

- Media list with contact names, address, e-mail, phone, and fax information
- Authorities list with contact names, address, e-mail, phone, and fax information
- Stakeholders list with contact names, address, e-mail, phone, and fax information
- Spokesperson list with contact names, address, e-mail, phone, and fax information
- Each of the above lists is stored on the M drive, a hard copy retained at the homes of spokespersons, and on CD located in the office vault, bank vault, and at the homes of spokespersons

Sub-team: Legal

The legal sub-team is charged with responding to legal issues related to the crisis and legal requirements for works in progress.

Contact Information

Name	Responsibility	Contact Information
	Team Leader	W: H: C: P:
	Team Member	W: H: C: P:
	Team Member	W: H: C: P:

Team Responsibilities

- Provide assistance to claims personnel, in particular professional liability claims, during the crisis
- Review any contracts or legal question that may arise
- Provide assistance to crisis management team and/or other units (e.g., HR) to determine any impacts on legal obligations to vendors, customers, regulatory units, and employees, and determine action needed to mitigate damages

Team Tasks

- Review and approve news releases
- Respond to requests from other teams regarding legal issues, contracts, etc.
- Arrange for works in progress with legal deadlines to be continued

Equipment/Supplies Required

- Table and chairs to seat two people
- One to two telephones (may be cell phones)
- Notebook PC
- ACD phones with headsets

Important Documents and Location

- Off-site storage: Box XYZ-789

Sub-team: HR/payroll

The HR/payroll sub-team is charged with accounting for employee's well-being, monitoring employee behavior, and payroll.

Contact Information

Name	Responsibility	Contact Information
	Team Leader	W: H: C: P:
	Team Member	W: H: C: P:
	Team Member	W: H: C: P:

Team Responsibilities

- Arrange for payroll
- Coordinate counseling services/employee assistance program (EAP) for employees and employees' families

Team Tasks

- Contact temporary agencies regarding any temporary employees working
- Coordinate employee notification of when and where to return to work
- Schedule debriefing meeting for non-recovery employees
- Distribute benefit handout at debriefing meeting
- Coordinate benefit communication to employees
- Prepare payroll by duplicating last payroll file

Equipment/Supplies Required

- Pens, paper
- Paper for printer
- Computer and laser jet legal size printer
- Table and three chairs
- Phone and/or cell phones

Important Documents and Location

- Benefit information handout; Personnel file cabinet #23
- Beneficiary forms—life insurance forms; located in four three-ring binders in overhead bin and 401(k) forms located in expandable file
- Gap pension files—HO files located on south wall in filing cabinet and field files located in filing cabinets on north wall

IT Team

The IT team is responsible for restoring critical hardware, software, and data within an established timeframe so that critical business function may resume.

Contact Information

Name	Responsibility	Contact Information
	Team Leader	W: H: C: P:
	Team Member	W: H: C: P:
	Team Member	W: H: C: P:

IT Team Responsibilities

- Supervise and coordinate activities of data processing, network, servers, telcom, and PC support sub-teams
- See sub-team lists

IT Team Tasks

- See sub-team lists

Equipment/Supplies Required

- See sub-team lists

Important Documents and Location

- See sub-team lists and inventory of off-site storage

Sub-team: Data Processing

The data processing sub-team is responsible for set up and verification that databases, SQL server databases, and other databases have been recovered and are up and operational and to troubleshoot any databases that did not come up.

Contact Information

Name	Responsibility	Contact Information
	Team Leader	W: H: C: P:
	Team Member	W: H: C: P:
	Team Member	W: H: C: P:

Team Responsibilities

- Verify that databases are ready to use.

Team Tasks

- Configure and test secondary data center servers.
- Work with the DBA administrators to possibly limit the incoming so as to not overwhelm our single database order taker.
- Assist the DBA administrators in setting up a primary database server to begin restoring our primary database to a different machine.

Equipment/Supplies Required

- PCs, phones, notebooks, pens, SSH software, Internet connectivity.

Important Documents and Location

- Duplicate of all manuals, SOPs, operating software CDs located at off-site storage bay one

Sub-team: Network

The network sub-team is responsible for LAN/WAN and Internet connectivity at the recovery site.

Contact Information

Name	Responsibility	Contact Information
	Team Leader	W: H: C: P:
	Team Member	W: H: C: P:
	Team Member	W: H: C: P:

Team Responsibilities

- Restoration of LAN infrastructure
- Recovery of computer room infrastructure
- Advise the command center of status and progress
- Ensure availability of necessary test equipment
- Ensure network data is properly backed up
- Coordinate the notification and restoration of services with network vendors
- Ensure that appropriate replacement equipment is ordered
- Periodically review and revise the Telcom/network equipment configuration
- Review plan, policies, and procedures; submit changes as required
- Coordinate with and assist other business units during planning and recovery
- Develop and execute exercise scenarios for all team responsibilities
- Train newly assigned team members

Team Tasks

- Identify equipment and software requirements for network and firewall systems

- Acquire and install all network equipment
- Restore data communications links between critical servers
- Establish data communications for critical applications
- Test network operations
- Restore communication to Internet
- Secure data and servers from sabotage

Equipment/Supplies Required

- Netware manuals
- Tape backup reports

Important Documents and Location

- Complete set of duplicate manuals, SOPs, operating software located at off-site storage bay one

Sub-team: Servers

This team is responsible for installing servers, software, and workstations as required. (See appendix F for system recovery processes.)

Contact Information

Name	Responsibility	Contact Information
	Team Leader	W: H: C: P:
	Team Member	W: H: C: P:
	Team Member	W: H: C: P:

Team Responsibilities

- Restore server files and databases
- Advise command center of status and progress
- Ensure that appropriate evaluations are performed on alternate processing systems
- Obtain/replace data communications equipment as necessary
- Validate and support applications and utility software as required
- Develop and execute exercise scenarios for all team responsibilities
- Train newly assigned team members
- Ensure proper SAN connectivity and synchronization

Team Tasks

- Coordinate equipment installation and configuration
- Restore server operating system and application files per server priority list
- Test restored system
- Notify team leader as to server restoration status on a periodic basis
- Connect to LAN at recovery site

- Attempt to retrieve lost or damaged data
- Restore hardware
- Restore operating and application software
- Install and test software at the backup site
- Restore, balance, and validate critical database and parameter files

Equipment/Supplies Required

- Access to Internet
- Access to LAN

Important Documents and Location

- Complete set of manuals, SOPs, and software stored in off-site storage bay two

Sub-team: Telcom

Telcom sub-team function: To establish telephone service for incoming calls group, to establish telephone and voice mail service to the business unit staff, and restore telephone service.

Contact Information

Name	Responsibility	Contact Information
	Team Leader	W: H: C: P:
	Team Member	W: H: C: P:
	Team Member	W: H: C: P:

Team Responsibilities

- Contact phone companies for recorded caller announcements if necessary
- Contact phone companies to move local, long distance, and toll-free circuits to the recovery site
- Contact phone systems vendor to supply equipment. If call manager and unity is used, contact support for programming of systems

Team Tasks

- Program telephone and phone mail systems in recovery site
- Install phones in the recovery site
- Program phone systems and install phones in recovery site
- Contact vendors to get phone equipment, connect local, long distance, toll-free circuits to recovery site. Program systems and install phones in recovery site

Equipment/Supplies Required

- Pads of paper, pens, pencils

- Two PCs to access call manager and unity or terminal attached to Seimens phone systems
- One cell phone

Important Documents and Location

- System schematics and equipment lists on CD and in hard copies at control desk in recovery site

Sub-team: PC Support

The PC support sub-team function is to build PCs to allow access to critical applications.

Contact Information

Name	Responsibility	Contact Information
	Team Leader	W: H: C: P:
	Team Member	W: H: C: P:
	Team Member	W: H: C: P:

Team Responsibilities

- Obtain PC hardware required for restoration of critical application access
- Restore PCs to allow access to critical applications
- Advise the command center of status and progress
- Provide ongoing support for PCs once they are operational

Team Tasks

- Coordinate with team leader to determine which critical applications need to be installed
- Throughout the process, inform the command center of the status of each PC setup with access to critical application
- Obtain PCs and network interfaces required for recovery
- Set up PCs for IT recovery staff
- Set up PCs for access to critical applications
- Provide ongoing support for PCs

Equipment/Supplies Required

- Standard inventory of PC parts (in storage off-site)
- PC rebuild scripts on CD Rom

Important Documents and Location

- PC rebuild scripts and standard inventory list are with parts at off-site storage

Logistics Team

The logistics team is charged with determining the status of damage to buildings and equipment, coordinating the movement of people, equipment, and supplies, retrieving backup tapes, CDs, and documents and delivering to the recovery site.

Contact Information

Name	Responsibility	Contact Information
	Team Leader	W: H: C: P:
	Team Member	W: H: C: P:
	Team Member	W: H: C: P:

Logistics Team Responsibilities

- Facilitate the ordering and delivery of required equipment and supplies
- Assess damage immediately after disaster

Logistics Team Tasks

- Arrange for supplies, food, and water
- Perform shipping and receiving functions
- Arrange transportation of personel, equipment, supplies, and lodging as required
- Request offsite storage vendor to move required items to recovery site
- Notify recovery site of disaster

Sub-team: Damage Assessment and Salvage

The damage assessment and salvage sub-team function is to assess the extent of the disaster, perform required salvage, and provide updates to disaster management team leaders through logistics team leader.

Contact Information

Name	Responsibility	Contact Information
	Team Leader	W: H: C: P:
	Team Member	W: H: C: P:
	Team Member	W: H: C: P:

Team Responsibilities

- Perform survey of damage to buildings and equipment
- Inform logistics team leader of status of damage to building and equipment/inventory stored in yard
- Identify salvageable material and equipment in building and yard

Team Tasks

- Conduct preliminary review of building to determine severity of damage
- Document severity of damage and record possible salvageable material and equipment
- Make recommendations on salvageable equipment or inventory
- Arrange loading and delivery of salvaged items, if needed, to alternate site

Equipment/Supplies Needed

- Camera
- Cell phone and walkie-talkie
- Hard hat w/light

- Protective clothing

Important Documents and Location

- Supplier contact list on CD and hard copy in file cabinet #3 at off-site storage

Sub-team: Supplier Contact

The supplier contact sub-team function is to notify outside suppliers and manage that ongoing communication.

Contact Information

Name	Responsibility	Contact Information
	Team Leader	W: H: C: P:
	Team Member	W: H: C: P:
	Team Member	W: H: C: P:

Team Responsibilities

- Contact suppliers as appropriate

Team Tasks

- Contact appropriate suppliers as needed (see appendix S for supplier list)
- Procure all requirements and monitor the acquisition process
- Arrange travel and lodging requirements needed for employees, contractors, or suppliers
- Arrange freight and logistics for salvaged and new material to alternate sites
- Document receipts and condition of purchased and salvaged material

Equipment/Supplies Needed

- Phone

Important Documents and Location

- Suppliers, addresses, phones, etc.; off-site storage file cabinet #3
- Hospitals listing; see appendix G regional information

Business Units Team

The business unit's team responsibilities are to maintain contact with customers and clients, administer financial affairs, and sustain efforts to restore normal operations.

Contact Information

Name	Responsibility	Contact Information
	Team Leader	W: H: C: P:
	Team Member	W: H: C: P:
	Team Member	W: H: C: P:

Business Units Team Responsibilities

- Supervise and coordinate the activities of accounting, sales, marketing, and finance sub-teams
- See sub-team lists

Business Units Team Tasks

- See sub-team lists

Equipment/Supplies Required

- See sub-team lists

Important Documents and Location

- See sub-team lists and inventory of off-site storage

Sub-Team: Accounting

The accounting sub-team is responsible for carrying out the defined team responsibilities and team tasks in the approved business continuity plan.

Contact Information

Name	Responsibility	Contact Information
	Team Leader	W: H: C: P:
	Team Member	W: H: C: P:
	Team Member	W: H: C: P:

Team Responsibilities

- Communicate to accounting employees instructions about where to go, when to go there, along with a list of phone numbers for updates and when to call those numbers
- Contact key suppliers, key customers, and federal agencies (e.g., Security and Exchange Commission) to make sure they understand the temporary working limitations due to the disaster
- Team leads will identify the critical documents at the disaster site that will need to be obtained by the logistics team
- Team leads will monitor the logistics team's success in obtaining critical documents
- Team leads will keep track of those critical functions that must be done at a particular time of day and if the deadline cannot be reached, to contact the client, keeping them informed of the progress in meeting that deadline

Team Tasks

- Determine at what point in the process work was lost and where a team's work stopped
- Recreate a list of customers that are on credit hold
- Review requirements for go-live work and prioritize tasks

- Call key suppliers, key customers, federal agencies, and service providers
- Submit request for printout of key system reports from the backup system

Equipment/Supplies Required

- Electric typewriter
- Company letterhead
- Envelopes for mailing receivable manual adjustments and manual checks for accounts payable and payroll
- Telephones for each team member
- Fax machines for each team member
- Computers with access to servers
- Desks, chairs, and calculators for each team member
- Dun and Bradstreet connection

Important Documents and Location

- Accounting backup files, accounts receivable credit memos, check copies, customer files, software CDs, and essential supplies located at off-site storage in bay four

Sub-team: Marketing

The marketing sub-team is charged with maintaining the integrity of overall marketing plans during crisis and ensuring the continuity of vendor and advertising relationships.

Contact Information

Name	Responsibility	Contact Information
	Team Leader	W: H: C: P:
	Team Member	W: H: C: P:
	Team Member	W: H: C: P:

Team Responsibilities

- All operations can be suspended during the first seventy-two hours of a disaster and up to a week or more if need be, per executives' decision
- Document vendor lists
- Document advertising and promotional schedules

Team Tasks

- Fielding and resolving complex service calls from distributors/chains
- Responding to account executive information and service requests
- Fielding inquiries from potential new chain/distributor accounts
- Compiling data to produce monthly and ad hoc reports
- Contacting vendors and ad representatives that have immediate issues/projects

Equipment/Supplies Required

- Phone

Important Documents and Location

- Backup packaging and advertising graphics located on CDs in file cabinet #5 in bay five with marketing department backup files

Sub-team: Sales

The sales sub-team function is charged with merchandising operations, labor, and after-sales processes.

Contact Information

Name	Responsibility	Contact Information
	Team Leader	W: H: C: P:
	Team Member	W: H: C: P:
	Team Member	W: H: C: P:

Team Responsibilities

- Ensure and maximize store productivity and operations.

Team Tasks

- Re-establish and maintain contact with sales managers

Equipment/Supplies Needed

- PC or laptop
- Phones
- Table and chairs
- Access to vendor management information

Important Documents and Location

- Backup files, including sales manager's list and vendor management information located in file cabinet #6 in off-site storage, bay five

Sub-team: Finance

The finance sub-team is responsible for payroll, accounts payable functions, the billing of special groups, cost and budget functions, processing premium payments, making bank deposits, and developing financial reports for the company.

Contact Information

Name	Responsibility	Contact Information
	Team Leader	W: H: C: P:
	Team Member	W: H: C: P:
	Team Member	W: H: C: P:

Team Responsibilities

- Ensure payroll gets completed
- Ensure accounts payable function continues to operate
- Process premium payments and make bank deposits
- Deposit cash receipts in a timely manner
- Ensure financial reporting function continues to operate

Team Tasks

- Process payroll if needed–print checks
- Process accounts payable functions
- Pay suppliers through accounts payable–print checks
- Process subscriber and group dues; make deposits
- Produce accounts receivable and billings–process their payments
- Produce financial reports as needed

Equipment/Supplies Required

- Three computers

- Telephone
- Printer for checks
- Three calculators
- Four desks with chairs

Important Documents and Location

- Backup files, CDs for operating software, bank deposit slips, limited supply of check stock for payroll and accounts payable functions located in off-site storage bay seven
- Additional check stock and bank deposit slips available from local bank

APPENDIX H

Sample Regional Information

Regional Information should include phone numbers for the following services:

AIRPORTS, AIR AND GROUND SERVICES

- Charter Air Service
- Helicopter Service

AMERICAN RED CROSS

AUTOMATIC TELLER INFORMATION

AUTOMOTIVE SERVICE STATIONS

CELLULAR PHONE SERVICES

CHAMBERS OF COMMERCE

CONFERENCE CENTERS

CONVENTION VISITORS BUREAU

COPY, PRINTING, AND DUPLICATING SERVICES

COURIER SERVICES

DAMAGE APPRAISAL AND RESTORATION

DAY CARE FACILITIES

EMERGENCY TELEPHONE NUMBERS

- Road Conditions
- Police, Fire, Emergency
- Emergency Vsat Vendors

FORMS SUPPLIERS

HEALTH CARE FACILITIES

- Hospitals
- Clinics
- Urgent Care Facilities

HOTELS AND MOTELS

INTERNATIONAL CURRENCY WIRING

LIBRARIES

LOST OR STOLEN CREDIT CARDS

American Express
AT&T Universal Card
Discover Card
MasterCard
VISA
Diner's Club

MEDIA REPAIRS: CONVERSIONS/RECOVERY

MICROFICHE SERVICES

MISCELLANEOUS SUPPLIERS

This would include:
Software Restoration Services
Power Conversion Services
Disaster Services
Fire/Water Damage Services

OFF-SITE STORAGE FACILITIES/STORAGE SUPPLIES

RESTAURANTS

SECURITY GUARD SERVICES

SHOPPING CENTERS

STAFFING SERVICES (DATA ENTRY)

SUPPLIES AND EQUIPMENT RENTAL

TRANSPORTATION SERVICES

Automobile and Truck Rentals
Bus Rental
Public Transportation
Trains

TRAVEL AGENCIES

U.S. POSTAL SERVICE

WEATHER

APPENDIX I

Notes

Notes

RESPONSE!

ABOUT THE AUTHOR

Robert C. Huber

Robert Huber is the founder and CEO of USG, Inc. a company specializing in emergency recovery planning for major corporations and government agencies at all levels. Clients include Motorola, General Dynamics, General Mills, Digital Globe, Wyeth Pharmaceuticals, Dakota County, City of Minneapolis, Minnesota State Colleges and Universities, and the MSP International Airport.

Huber has over twenty years experience in risk assessment, emergency response, business continuity planning and training, along with a lifetime career in emergency management. He is a highly decorated veteran police officer and investigator who earned several department commendation awards during his assignment in uniformed district patrol. During his career in law enforcement, he graduated top in his class at the FBI Academy in Quantico, Virginia, where he later served as an adjunct instructor. He later graduated from ATF School and the IRS Criminal Investigator School where he also later served as an instructor. After completing special secret service training, he was assigned as a bodyguard for the Vice President of the United States.

Mr. Huber is a nationally recognized authority in emergency response and recovery and has been quoted in the *Wall Street Journal*, *Time* Magazine, *Computerworld*, NBC, CBS, ABC, *US* Magazine, *Bottomline*, *PC Week*, *Corporate Report Minnesota*, *Minnesota Technology*, *USA Today*, as well as in textbooks on computer crime.

www.ingramcontent.com/pod-product-compliance
Lightning Source LLC
Chambersburg PA
CBHW051457170526
45166CB00001B/279

* 9 7 8 1 4 9 2 3 5 5 5 0 2 *